HOMEMAKING HANDBOOK

a practical guide to managing home and family without losing yourself

Alina Lauren

ALINA LAUREN

Copyright © 2018 Prism Perfect Publications All rights reserved.

No part of this publication may be reproduced, distributed, or transmitted in any form or by any means, including photocopying, recording, or other electronic or mechanical methods, without the prior written permission of the publisher, except in the case of brief quotations embodied in reviews and certain other non-commercial uses permitted by copyright law.

ISBN: 9781790486953

DEDICATION

I would like to dedicate this book to the following people:

My Parents
My mother has always wanted the best for me, and throughout her life strived to bless me and my brothers with everything we needed to succeed. Mom and Dad, thank you for always supporting me and encouraging me to follow my dreams.

My Husband
My husband has supported me through every step in my mothering journey. I have been blessed with a husband who loves me, inspires me, and pushes me to be more than I ever thought possible. Sam, I love you so much and I will forever be grateful for your presence in my life.

TABLE OF CONTENTS

DEDICATION I

TABLE OF CONTENTS II

ACKNOWLEDGMENTS VI

DOWNLOAD THE FREE WORKBOOK III

PART 1 : INTRODUCTION **1**

1 : PREPARING TO PARENT 3

So Where Do We Start? 4

Bridging the Gap...7

The End Goal..9

Reflection Questions 11

2 : THE HATS YOU WEAR 13

Housekeeper..16

Chef..18

Taxi Driver and Chauffeur...19

Nurse 20

Playmate..21

Teacher..22

Secretary..23

Conclusion..24

Reflection Questions 26

3 : BALANCING THE ELEMENTS 27

Physical Wellness...28

Emotional Wellness 30

Intellectual Wellness...31

Social Wellness 31

Occupational Wellness...32

Environmental Wellness...32

Spiritual Wellness 33

Financial Wellness 33

Tying It All Together 34

Reflection Questions 35

4 : BREAK IT DOWN 37

Part II : Home...38

Part III : Family...39

Part IV : Self 40
Types of Imbalance 41
Reflection Questions 49

PART 2 : HOME **51**

5 : ORDER AND ORGANIZATION 53
Cleaning 54
Scheduling 56
Budgeting 57
Action Plan 60
6 : HEALTH 61
Exercise 62
Meal Planning 63
Nutrition 67
Gardening 68
Hygiene 69
Action Plan 71
7 : HAPPY HOME 73
Family Night 74
Activity Stations 75
Applying the List.. 77
Do Good 77
Action Plan 79

PART 3 : FAMILY **81**

8 : FAMILY UNITY.. 83
Family Purpose.. 85
Creating a Vision 85
Family Dinners.. 88
Family Councils.. 88
The Family Council 88
Couple Council.. 89
Couple & Kids Council.. 89
Parent & Child Council.. 89
Action Plan 91
9 : HUSBAND.. 93
People Priorities 94
Structure of Support.. 95

Responsibilities 96

Action Plan 99

10 : CHILDREN 101

Hard Work and Responsibility 102

School 104

Their Dreams 107

Action Plan 109

11 : EXTENDED FAMILY AND FRIENDS 111

Cleave 112

Let Them Fade 114

Party On 115

Action Plan 117

PART 4 : SELF **119**

12 : PREFACE 121

Self Focus > Selfishness 123

Work Your Family In 124

Be Supported 125

Action Plan 127

13 : THE POWER HOUR TECHNIQUE 129

Making It Work 131

Time and Support From Your Spouse 133

Use Your Time Well 134

Action Plan 137

14 : THE EIGHT ELEMENTS 139

Physical 140

Emotional 141

Intellectual 142

Social 143

Occupational 144

Environmental 145

Spiritual 146

Financial 148

Action Plan 150

PART 5 : CONCLUSION **151**

15 : MASTER PLAN 153

1 : Goals 153

2 : Schedule	154
3 : Responsibilities	154
4 : Get Clean	154
5 : Budget	155
6 : Meal Plan	155
7 : Organize	155
8 : Reach Out	155
9 : Repeat	156
16 : YOU ARE UNIQUE	157
The Perfect Mother	159
The Key Element	160
ABOUT THE AUTHOR	163

ACKNOWLEDGMENTS

Alden Dean
For delicious dinners and
memorable soccer games.

Alannah Birkinsha
For organizing an awesome book
club with a pleasant personality.

Amy Dampt
For raising my husband and
helping me learn French.

Blair Torres
For helping me survive and enjoy
high school/college.

Brianna Orgill
For writing music with me and
being my best friend.

Cynthia Merrill
For being a wonderful and
insightful editor.

Heidi Brubaker
For being an amazing example of
a patient and loving mother.

Hika Cooper
For marrying my brother and
being a cook I can count on.

Jessica Black
For her charming personality and
lovely, unique peg doll creations.

Julia Staples
For encouraging your brother to
marry me, and being my sister.

Karli Denton
For your fearlessness in standing
up for what is right.

Lauren Thibaudeau
For being my best friend and
bringing excitement in my life.

LeeAnn Spencer
For bringing out the crazy in me
and always supporting me.

Maddie Flake
For being my go-to hairstylist
and closest cousin.

Manon Dampt
For being an awesome sister and
"Just Dance" partner.

Melissa Fitzgerald
For being my dance team
partner-in-crime.

Sharon Bond
For being my strongest support
system through my wedding.

Shelisa Baldwin
For helping me survive life as a
Law School Spouse.

Tess Prince
For being willing and proactive in
the book launch process.

And for their immense support in the book launch process:

Melany Fuller

Kristen Gardner

Antonia Ricks

Marina Reidhead

Kelsey Sorenson

Lina Felix

Megan Collins

Aubrey Hartshorn

Shannon Thevenin

Tawnyel Perkes

Rachel Northrup

ii

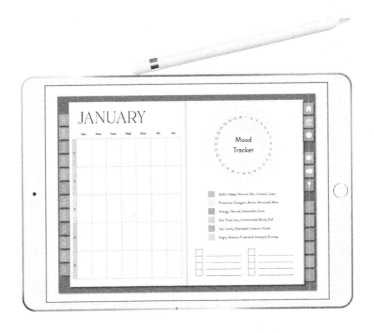

DOWNLOAD THE FREE DIGITAL PLANNER

Read this First

As a special thank you for purchasing my book, I'd like to offer you a free printable planner that can be used aside this book 100% FREE!

To download go to:

https://alinadampr.com/tools

PART 1: INTRODUCTION

2

1 : PREPARING TO PARENT

Try to think back on one of the most memorable and beautiful days of your life. This could be your wedding day, your first date with your future spouse, or the birth of your first child. My wedding day was one of the most beautiful and memorable days of my life. Second in line would be my first daughter's birth, and I'm sure every child's birth that follows will fall into the same beautiful and memorable category.

Think back to your wedding day, or the birth of any of your children. Those were memorable moments. Likely, they are most memorable because they are the beginning of a new chapter in your life. You were embarking on a new adventure.

New adventures can be so exciting, but the days that follow can be excruciating. Take your wedding for example: during the first few days and even weeks, the experience can be glorious. Then over time, you start noticing that living with another human with their own ideas and habits can be frustrating, confusing, and even anger-inducing at times.

Don't get me wrong, I love my husband, but there is a learning curve for everyone! You have to balance chores, financial obligations, quality time with each other, and more as real life sets in. That honeymoon phase ends eventually.

The same can happen with a new baby's birth. When our first daughter was born, my husband and I would stay up late into the night as we tried to find a way to balance our relationship with each other and our new relationships with our daughter. I was an emotional crying mess, and it was a whole new learning curve!

Becoming a wife and a mother is one of those big steps into a new world. I had a rough time of it. Most difficult for me was the process of learning that my ambitions and hopes and dreams were no longer the top priority. Likewise, everything I had learned up to that point, everything I had been taught was most important, all flew way out the window when it came to motherhood.

So Where Do We Start?

I have included two tables in this section, just to give us an idea of what our childhood prepares us for. First, I want to review some classes we've enjoyed in our education up to this point. These are your basic classes that are required or encouraged in all schools:

English	Social Studies
<ul><li>Literature</li><li>Writing and Composition</li><li>Speech</li></ul>	<ul><li>US Government</li><li>US History</li><li>World History</li><li>Geography</li></ul>
Mathematics	Science
<ul><li>Algebra</li><li>Geometry</li><li>Trigonometry</li><li>Calculus and Statistics</li></ul>	<ul><li>Biology</li><li>Chemistry</li><li>Physics</li><li>Earth or Space Sciences</li></ul>
Other	
<ul><li>Foreign Language</li><li>Arts</li><li>Computers</li></ul>	<ul><li>Physical Education</li><li>Psychology</li><li>Health</li></ul>

We may also have had great opportunities to explore some extracurricular activities. These could be sports, the arts, or any number of things that interested us. Growing up, my life was busy! I think most children have busy lives. A day in my life would have looked a lot like this:

5 a.m.	Wake up
6 a.m.	Early bird class
7:12 a.m.	School starts
1:15 p.m.	School ends
1:15-2 p.m.	Dance Team
2:30 p.m.	Snack at home
3:30 p.m.	Studio Dance classes begin
5:30 p.m.	Studio Dance classes end
6 p.m.	Dinner
6:30 p.m.	Homework until…
8 p.m.	Bedtime Routine

Then the next morning I would repeat the cycle more or less. To put it simply, learning was a huge factor in my life and I was always busy improving myself. This is not an unusual schedule or childhood. In fact, this has become the norm in America. Childhood is focused on learning, which is GREAT! But what are we learning, and what is it preparing us for?

ADULTING.

This new word has become more and more commonplace among my generation. It seems to accompany this underlying joke that basically no teen entering adulthood has any idea how to manage life's complexities. Unfortunately, beneath this joke is a truth: children are not being taught HOW to be adults in today's society.

When do children learn about paying taxes or buying a house? When do they learn about homemaking and changing a tire?

Budgeting? Cooking? Insurance? Applying for jobs? Building a résumé? Raising a family? Having a successful marriage?

Bridging the Gap

I believe that the rising generation of parents have been left at somewhat of a disadvantage entering adulthood. I like to call it the "self-to-selfless debacle." As a child, teenager, and even a young adult, we are very much focused on ourselves. We are focused on "my money, my education, my sleep, my food, my room/apartment, my job," and the list goes on.

Suddenly, we get married and each of these things turns into ours. Suddenly, we have to become selfless. We have another person to think about. Then add a child to the mix, and we are drowning in a need to be selfless, just to keep our offspring alive!

How do we bridge this gap? Going from thinking only of self to becoming selfless without losing yourself along the way. We have three sources to look to:

A. Our Parents

It is possible that we have really great examples that we have looked up to our entire lives. Hopefully, our parents are happily married and succeeding at this "adulting" thing. Some of us have not experienced this, but we have other couples that we know and respect. In each relationship we come across, we can find different accomplishments within them that resonate with us. Unfortunately, we do not really know how they got there, but we at least know what we would like the end result of our marriage (or relationship with our children) to look like.

B. Trial & Error

If you have been married for any length of time, you know that a lot of relationship fixes come about because of trial and error. You or your spouse makes a mistake, the other spouse struggles with being frustrated (there is possibly an outburst), and then finally the opposite spouse realizes they have been doing something wrong throughout the entire marriage.

Same goes for a lot of "adulting" we have to do. I can't tell you how many times I have tried mastering my chef skills and I still feel that I have nothing to show for it! Sometimes I make a schedule that will "work" and by the end of the week that schedule is completely forgotten and I am back to just surviving.

C. Educating Ourselves

This seems to be the last resort for many people. Although some people come into marriage prepared, I have found that the more I try and fail, the more likely I am to seek out a self-help book. (Is that why you're here?) I tend to reach a point where I would just like an answer. I want to know how to fix my bad habits NOW. I want someone to tell me what I am doing wrong so that I can fix it and be 100X less miserable.

Ladies, I want to be clear. This book is not a quick fix for mothers or wives. This book will not fix all of your problems overnight. This book will not give you insider knowledge to the ways of being a "perfect mom."

This book is more than that.

The End Goal

This book is about mastery. Not perfection. As I am sure you are all aware, perfection is impossible. I am not selling you some kind of magical, make-believe life with no heartache. With this book, you will have the tools to accomplish three very important things:

MASTERY

You will master motherhood. Mastery, in the dictionary, is defined as the "command or grasp, as of a subject." A master is "a person eminently skilled in something." Mastery is not perfection. Even masters of trades or talents make mistakes, but they know to pick themselves up and keep pressing forward. They know they have the tools to make them capable of working towards perfection, but they understand that there will always be ways to improve.

This will be you! You will have a clearer picture of how to get where you would like to go. You will have the tools to improve and press forward. You will master motherhood.

CONFIDENCE

You will gain confidence. We should not feel incapable of succeeding at the trade of motherhood. Since the dawn of time, women have been mothers and have succeeded as mothers, each in their own way. Each woman is unique and offers her own value to her family. You will find that through your unique qualities, dreams, and talents you can make a difference in the lives of your husband and your children.

A PLAN FOR YOUR FAMILY

You will be able to make a plan that will work for YOUR family. Your plan for being a successful mother will not look like my plan, your mother's plan, your sister's plan, or your best friend's plan. Your family is as unique as you are.

This might come as a surprise, but your husband is not exactly like your father, and you are not exactly like your mother. Furthermore, your children will be nothing like you were as a child. Are there basic rules for running a family that will apply? Yes. But beyond those basic rules, your role as a wife and mother will be very different from other women's.

Without further ado, let's jump into the next chapter and learn about the hats that a mother wears, and how each of these hats applies to you!

THE HOMEMAKING HANDBOOK

REFLECTION QUESTIONS

What talents do you feel you have built up over the course of your childhood?

What abilities do you find you are lacking in?

What "adulting" skills make you uncomfortable?

What "adulting" skills do you feel you have mastered?

What has helped you bridge the gap between childhood and adulthood?

What would you like to accomplish as a wife and mother?

12

2 : THE HATS YOU WEAR

There are many Facebook posts, memes, and blog posts talking about all of the jobs that a woman fulfills as a mother. Here are just a few: taxi driver, chef, nurse, counselor, cheerleader, housekeeper, and teacher. Although these posts are generally well-intentioned, I think they can set a dangerous precedent for our mindsets as a mother, and I'd like to address two mindset changes that will be integral to your success in balancing these responsibilities in your life.

Pride —> Responsibility

Unfortunately, I feel like a lot of these posts regarding the hats we wear as mothers are used to bash others over the head with ideas of motherhood superiority. I want to encourage you as a mother to, instead of gleaning pride from the work you're expected to do as a mother, recognize that this means you have responsibilities.

Remember that holding a title does not entitle anyone to praise, it entitles them to responsibilities.

Let's look at a simple example. There have been a myriad of good and bad leaders in countries over the course of history. They all held the "title" of either president, prime minister, king, or maybe emperor. Holding these titles didn't make these individuals good at the responsibilities of said career. Simply compare Winston Churchill and Hitler.

There's a really good idiom in French about this point, and in English it translates to:

The clothes don't make the man.

As mother, we can carry many titles. But a good thing to keep in mind is that 'the clothes don't make the (wo)man.' What do I mean by that? Simply carrying a title (cook, for example) doesn't make you a good cook.

In the same way, holding the title of "mother" doesn't make an individual naturally good at organizing and implementing the responsibilities of a mother. However, mastering motherhood responsibilities can be learned, and anyone who strives to be good at managing their time, talents, and abilities to serve others, grow, and improve will naturally find that praise follows their efforts. Our focus, as mothers, should be on managing the responsibilities associated with the title of "mother." The praise will follow as we shift our focus to growing and improving.

Why is it so integral that we shift our focus to our responsibilities instead of receiving praise? The answer is simple. Focusing on the responsibilities we have will encourage us to notice where we fall a little short and give us a blueprint to change and improve. If we take the prideful approach and focus on the praise we want to be receiving then our ability to improve will stall, as well as our progress, and keep us from achieving the balance we're looking for.

The second mindset change we need to address is:

Overwhelm —> Taking Control

The other impact that the "hats of a mother" idea has is to overwhelm mothers who feel they are incapable of filling all of these roles. Let's be clear, being a mother doesn't mean you need to be a superior chef, experienced nurse, and seasoned taxi driver. Being a mother simply means you will need to develop basic skills in these "career paths."

In this chapter we will be doing a quick overview of some of these "hats." I want you to understand your sweet spot for these responsibilities. You, as a mother, will probably often feel like you are underperforming. (I know that I regularly feel that way.) But as long as you can hit a sweet spot that works for your family, in understanding these responsibilities as a mother, then you are doing well!

Your mindset over the course of this book should shift from a feeling of being overwhelmed to confidence in the ability to take control of the responsibilities you have as a mother. Just remember, these hats and responsibilities are not your full-time job. They are not even a part-time job.

Let me give you a quick example: One of your children, at some point in your life, may insist on a three-course meal for dinner. REMEMBER: your child is not paying for your services as a waitress, chef, and dishwasher at a 5-star restaurant. Your only responsibility as a mother is to make sure your child is fed and healthy. Your title is not chef, it is mother, thus your responsibilities should reflect that.

Being a mother does require certain responsibilities related to the basic responsibilities in many career paths. Over the next few sections I am going to lay out a framework for you to refer to for some of these "hats." This chapter will give you an overview of the responsibilities that you need to be aware of. Through Parts 2, 3, and 4 of this book we will address how you can take control of these responsibilities.

Housekeeper

Every homemaker knows this is one of their biggest responsibilities. Heaven knows, kids are a mess. (Sometimes husbands are too.) Although it may seem daunting, maintaining a clean and organized house doesn't need to be stressful. You can acquire help for a lot of these responsibilities through the download offered at the beginning of this book, as well as through online searches, books, and more.

Every family's cleaning needs will be different in small ways. My first daughter was notorious for throwing food off of her high chair as she ate. This meant that meal after meal I had to schedule time for a quick sweep and spot mop of the area surrounding her chair. Will this be necessary for you? I hope not! But you will definitely find that your family's quirks force certain countermeasures in the cleaning department.

Your Responsibilities:

- Organizing and recognizing household chores
- Understanding the basics of general chores: vacuuming, sweeping, mopping, dishes, taking out the trash, laundry, tidying up, cleaning toilets, and more.
- Delegating chores and creating chore charts
- Organizing and implementing a workable maintenance schedule
- Organizing the spaces in your home to avoid clutter
- Asking for help when you need it

NOT Your Responsibilities:

- Having a spotless house every time guests arrive
- Managing all cleaning responsibilities alone
- Scrubbing your shower an hour a day
- Vacuuming every five minutes
- Cleaning the grout with a toothbrush

Chef

The kitchen necessities of any mother can be boiled down to basic kitchen supplies, a collection of simple recipes, and a meal planning calendar (which I highly encourage for money, time, and energy-saving purposes.) You can find recipes online or in recipe books at the store. When mastering your chef responsibilities, you may find there is some trial and error in creating a plan, but over time the effort now will make a huge difference later.

Early on in my marriage I had a goal to try a new recipe almost every night. (This was a really bad idea.) Not only was this expensive so early in our marriage, it also meant I had to spend a lot of time experimenting every night. Trying new recipes every once in a while is great, but, as a mother, you shouldn't feel expected to apply that creativity to every meal.

Your Responsibilities:

- Grocery shopping
- Organizing your pantry and fridge to reflect your meals
- Planning meals ahead to avoid wasting time, money, and resources
- Basic cooking
- Reading and following a recipe
- Knowing how to measure ingredients
- Understanding how to use the appliances in your kitchen
- Time management when cooking

- Understanding basic nutrition

NOT Your Responsibilities:
- Owning an expensive set of kitchen appliances
- Trying a new recipe every night
- Cooking extensive, difficult meals regularly
- 5 years of training at a culinary school
- An apron that would make Julia Child jealous

Taxi Driver and Chauffeur

A lot of your efforts will be spent coordinating each of your family member's schedules and measuring the times of departure for drop-offs and pick-ups. This will include loading everyone in the car, making sure you have enough gas, and knowing the routes to and from your destinations. Also, having a trustworthy car is important. Safety is important. Keeping up with the Joneses… not as important. Your car needs to get you safely from A to B. You need enough gas. It is that simple.

As your children get older, they may wish to receive rides to and from friend's homes or social activities. You will need to assess the plausibility of each social request and decide whether it is the best option for you and your family. Sometimes we have to say "no" to our children because of scheduling conflicts or simply because we are exhausted and we need to relax. This is part of your job as a mother.

Your Responsibilities:

- Have a driver's license
- Know how to get gas
- Have a basic knowledge of the geography of your town or a good GPS device
- Have a basic knowledge of your vehicle
- Know when to change the oil
- Know how to change a tire
- Be able to organize and schedule appointments and activities
- Know how to say "no" to activities

NOT Your Responsibilities

- Owning a brand new vehicle
- Being on call for rides
- Being a mechanic

Nurse

Believe it or not, accidents happen; someone in your family will get injured. It is a great idea to have a basic understanding of first aid, and to be prepared, should an emergency arise.

My husband and I, after being married for a month, had a major incident that I was not prepared for. My husband was making us a salad in the kitchen and chopping up an avocado, and suddenly I heard something of a scream... or a manly yell. Of course, I rushed out of the bathroom to the kitchen where my husband was holding his hand and kind of in shock. I see a knife and a half cut avocado on the counter. The avocado had slipped as he tried to remove the pit and he had almost sliced all the way through the palm of his hand. We had no first aid kit, so I made up for it by putting a paper towel over his hand and taping it with green and pink flowered washi tape. Not my proudest moment as a wife, but I did learn some lessons early on about being prepared!

Your Responsibilities:
- Having a basic knowledge of drugs, home remedies, and questionable symptoms
- Buying a first aid kit
- Kissing boo-boos
- Knowing when a sickness or injury is out of your hands and it's time to seek professional help

NOT Your Responsibilities:
- 3 years of med school
- A nursing degree

Playmate

Our kids need our attention. Honestly, I think this is one of the most important jobs a parent has, especially a mother at home. New toys are cool, but your love is most important!

If you are a seasoned mother, you may have learned that every new toy only gets so much attention before it is tossed to the side. With my oldest child my husband and I found ourselves shopping for a new toy every week, just to find something to entertain her for five minutes. Over time, we stopped making purchases and started handing out daughter spoons, bowls, and miscellaneous household items. For young mothers, do not waste your time building up a huge toy collection. You will find that most of your purchases are in vain.

Your Responsibilities:

- Taking time for your kid
- Putting your phone away
- Being creative about activities at home
- Encouraging a range of activities to be explored

NOT Your Responsibilities:

- A completely stocked, high-end playroom
- Buying every new toy that your child shows interested in
- Finding entertainment for your child 24/7

Teacher

We are the primary educators for our children, especially before they start school. Some of us even challenge ourselves a little differently and choose to homeschool. I will mention homeschooling in later chapters, but the focus of your role as a teacher in this book will revolve around your early learners.

Teaching your children should be fun! Learning is fun until it becomes a chore. Help your children love learning and they will succeed throughout their lives.

Your Responsibilities:

- Working with your child to learn to talk, walk, and use the potty
- Reading books and going to the library
- Answering the "why" questions
- Helping your children discover new hobbies and interests

NOT Your Responsibilities:

- Owning a blackboard/whiteboard
- Having superior knowledge in all subjects
- Obtaining a teaching degree

Secretary

Almost all paperwork from school, extracurricular activities, and events passes through your hands. You have to be able to stay on top of all of this information to avoid making late payments, missing permission slips, or forgetting important appointments. Your ability to organize your home and family life is the main priority because this is what will keep you sane. This hat will be covered more than any other hat in the book. Be prepared to take notes and implement strategies!

Your family may be different, but if scheduling was left up to my husband then we'd never make it out of the house for events, appointments, and basic needs. Since the beginning of our marriage I even bought a white board calendar showcasing every little thing we need to be aware of. The trick has been convincing my husband that he needs to actually look at it every once in a while. Regardless, we've found our own way to make it work, just as you will with your family!

Your Responsibilities:

- Scheduling appointments
- Keeping track of events
- Budgeting
- Organization
- Paperwork

NOT Your Responsibilities:

- Experience as a secretary

Conclusion

Although we won't cover all of these responsibilities in great depth, we will touch on most of them. If you ever find yourself struggling with a responsibility that is not covered in depth in this book you can reach out to other women who seem to have the skills, take a class, look up a YouTube channel, buy a book, and more. In this day and age, we have so many free and cheap resources at our disposal that growth and improvement can be a relatively simple process.

By now, I hope you are feeling a lot better! Of course, there are many more hats that mothers wear, but these are the ones that you will want to learn the basic skills from. Often we are hard on ourselves as mothers and we start to expect more out of ourselves than anyone is capable of. Remember that our goals over the course of this book are to change two mindsets:

Pride → Responsibility

&

Overwhelm → Taking Control

We are approaching this book in a hope to balance our lives. We've discussed the responsibilities that we are learning to balance and we are now going to cover the eight elements of wellness. These eight elements will play a part in our balancing act as mothers, and I will refer to them regularly over the course of this book!

REFLECTION QUESTIONS

Which hats do you feel you already wear proudly?

What hats are you afraid to put on and push forward in?

What hats are you more willing to delegate to someone else if you feel you have too much on your plate?

Who could you count on to delegate each hat to?
Your spouse? Your parents? Your oldest child?

3 : BALANCING THE ELEMENTS

One way to measure how "well" we are is by looking at the eight elements of wellness. These elements are essentially meant to break your life up into a spectrum where we can discover our strengths and weaknesses. I want you to remember these facets of wellness because I will be referring back to them regularly over the course of the book. Compartmentalizing our lives in this way will help us see where we can take better care of our home, our family, and ourselves; we will also see where we are succeeding.

The 8 Elements of Wellness:

- Physical
- Emotional
- Intellectual

- Social

- Occupational

- Environmental

- Spiritual

- Financial

What we are looking for is balance in all things. Let's illustrate it this way: if you are in really great shape, but are homeless, broke, and alone then there is obviously SOMETHING missing. Or maybe a few things.

I am going to break down each of these elements one-by-one so that we can discover the get a deeper look into how they affect our lives. What does it mean to be balanced between all of these elements? What does it mean to master just one of these elements?

Let's find out.

Physical Wellness

Physical wellness gets a lot of attention on social media. Every wife and mother is at a different place in their physical wellness journey. Some women struggle with improving their diets, but they enjoy a good run. Some hate exercising, but they take great care of their skin! There are three pieces to being physically well that we will cover: exercise, diet, and hygiene. These pieces are all part of the physical wellness puzzle, and we will discuss each of them over the course of the book.

A. EXERCISE

Physical activity is so important in our lives, but sometimes we feel like we do not have the time for it. Sometimes say we are too tired. Sometimes we just do not want to do it. However, I can assure you that to feel good every day, exercise is vital.

A lot of times exercise is presented simply for its aesthetic value. Think of every commercial you have seen for a fitness product. They always promise that "you will look like this if you use our product." Looking good is great, but being in shape is way more than that. Being in shape is having the energy to chase your toddler around. Being in shape makes a difference in how long we will live to enjoy our family, our children, and our grandchildren. Being in shape gives us the tools to participate in family outings, to go hiking, rocking climbing, and more.

B. DIET

I want to go beyond a healthy diet for families and mothers in this book. Yes, we will talk about nutrition, but there is more! How can we meal plan to save time and money? What can we grow at home? How do we organize our meals? What time do we have meals? When should I go grocery shopping?

Every family will be a little different, but there are some fun tricks to getting things just right for your family.

C. HYGIENE

This is the hardest one for me! Not because I am a messy, dirty slob, but because I have trouble finding time to put myself together. How many mothers have completely lost the willpower, time, and energy to worry about makeup and doing their hair every day? I have become a master at the ponytail, and I manage to get foundation on every day. For a long time, beyond those two things, I could not really manage much.

How can we get over this slump and find ways to make our morning and night routines work so that we can look as good as we feel? We'll learn tricks to this in later chapters.

Emotional Wellness

Emotional wellness is tied very strongly to the other elements. Emotional health is impacted by the other elements and fluctuates a TON! If we were going to simplify emotional wellness, we might describe it as "self-care," which, although not a new practice, has definitely seen more attention in recent years.

Self-care can include reading a book, going out with friends, writing in your journal, or watching a funny movie. It can be a number of things that can be applied to all seven other elements, but we are going to refer to this as "you time."

Emotional wellness is about rejuvenating yourself. Mothers do not get a lot of time to themselves; in fact, parents in general do not get a lot of time to themselves. We're going to cover some ways to make that time a reality.

Intellectual Wellness

Intellectual wellness is different from your education. You have the ability to learn new things every day. You do not have to be in a school environment to do so. In fact, some of the things we learn best are those passions that we delve into on our own time. Learning does not end with motherhood.

I have to admit that I struggled with this a lot when I first got married. I had my bachelor's degree in Dance Production and Management, and I was finished with school and ready to be a mom. Over time I realized that I felt really stagnant. I wanted to be learning new things and exploring new interests or improving on my already accomplished talents.

Up until I was married I took 18–24 credits every semester in college. I was not used to learning nothing. I felt like I needed a checklist so I could check off accomplishments as I went.

We'll discuss some ideas to be intellectually "well," even if you are not pursuing an education.

Social Wellness

I have to be honest—in general, I could not care less about my social life. I am an extremely private person, and spending time with my close family is about as much socializing as I need. I also recognize that this is not true for everyone. For some people, this is their rejuvenating emotional boost! (Do you see how other elements can impact your emotional health?)

One thing that has been difficult to figure out with kids has been date nights between my spouse and me. Do you have the same problem? Finding a babysitter, deciding what to do, fitting it into the budget: there are so many factors that simply become overwhelming.

We will discuss your relationship with your spouse, children, extended family, and more. Married life is truly a new world. Single life is so much simpler. We will talk about some of the changes, and help you make a plan to improve your relationships.

Occupational Wellness

Occupational wellness is a weird one, especially if you are a stay-at-home. There will be a large variation in different mothers' occupational wellness because it is situation specific. Sometimes the family's necessities require that mom takes on some work to help pay the bills, sometimes the family owns and runs a business, and sometimes our own ambitions lead us to create projects or build companies (much like this book was a project for me!).

No matter the reason, we have to find ways to fit in our work time without diminishing the value of the time we spend with our family. This is possible and it can be accomplished, and there is no need to feel guilty! We'll discuss this plenty in later chapters.

Environmental Wellness

There are two very different definitions of this topic: the world's definition and my own definition. The world's definition is very much related to recycling, taking care of the earth, and riding bikes instead of driving cars. Now, as a human being living on the earth, there is no reason you cannot stand up for these causes, but for the purposes of this book, it is less applicable.

My definition relates more to YOUR living environment. Is your house clean? How hard is it to keep up with the chores? Do you feel organized? Can you find anything you need in a flash because it has a place, or do you spend more time searching for lost things than actually using the lost thing?

Spiritual Wellness

When I first started studying the 8 elements of wellness I tied spiritual and emotional wellness to each other and had trouble differentiating the two, but I have come to a conclusion. Emotional wellness is about our emotions. Spiritual wellness is our sense of purpose. This is our WHY? Why am I seeking out a balance in my life? Why do I want to learn to paint? Why does any of this make a difference?

Most of your spiritual wellness journey in this book will relate to planning and goal-making. It will be the foundation of what makes you different from me. It will be what makes you an individual.

Spirituality can also relate to our relationship with a higher being. For you this may be God, the universe, or a large community. Beyond simply finding the answers to your "why?" questions, you may find a way to feel like you are a part of something greater than yourself.

Financial Wellness

I think that financial wellness should speak for itself. Finding financial peace will involve getting out of debt, setting up a working budget, and communicating with your husband about finances.

There is a reason that this is one of the leading causes of divorce, but it need not be an issue for you. Clear communication, expectations, and sympathy can go a LONG way! We will discuss this throughout the book as well.

Tying It All Together

I will point out specific practices and actions throughout this book to help you see what elements in life you are learning to balance. We will not take these in a step-by-step fashion. Instead, we will approach your motherhood journey in 3 basic categories that you are juggling as a mother, and show you that through the 8 elements you can balance all these aspects of your life.

THE HOMEMAKING HANDBOOK

REFLECTION QUESTIONS

On a scale from 1 to 10 how healthy do you feel in each element?

Physical?

Emotional?

Intellectual?

Social?

Occupational?

Environmental?

Spiritual?

Financial?

On a scale from 1 to 10, which elements are you most looking forward to improving?

Physical?

Emotional?

Intellectual?

Social?

Occupational?

Environmental?

Spiritual?

Financial?

36

4 : BREAK IT DOWN

Before we jump into the meat of this book I want you to see the big picture. What are all of the pieces that we are trying to balance to make ourselves and our family happy? To make it simple, I have broken it into 3 pieces.

HOME
FAMILY
SELF

These pieces are interwoven and connected in a million different ways, but they do need to be addressed separately. How you manage your home will affect your family relationships as well as your own well-being. How you handle yourself will affect your family and home. How you treat your family will affect you, and in turn your home environment.

It might seem like there is no way to organize all of these separate pieces, but I assure you there is. Bear with me!

Part II : Home

First, I want to delve into your responsibility as a homemaker. I am going to give you the simple definition and we will build from there:

Homemaker: A person, especially a housewife, who manages a home.

WOW! Guess what? There are no specific guidelines for how this needs to be done. There are no hard and fast rules, just the simple statement that you "manage the home." So, if you manage your home affairs, you have already got this in the bag.

However, you are probably reading this book because you believe that you are not doing it quite right or you just cannot figure out the secret to running everything smoothly. That is okay! We are going to go through some tips, tricks, and practices that can help you feel on top of your tasks.

As a homemaker, you cover 3 basic tasks: housekeeping, maintenance, and management.

Housekeeping generally refers to cooking, cleaning, and (the ever piling) laundry. These are chores and cleaning that need to get done at regular intervals to ensure the home is healthy.

Maintenance refers to larger equipment repairs and bigger jobs. This can be anything from adhering to HOA requirements to predicting when maintenance will need to be done to avoid catastrophes.

Management includes home organization. This could be anything from an aesthetically pleasing interior design to a daily act of de-cluttering. It also includes home purchases, such as groceries or clothing. Think secretarial work in the home.

In Chapter 5 we are going to cover ideas and plans for finding order and organization in your home. Chapter 6 will also discuss health and your role in the family's decisions regarding meals, exercise, and more. Lastly, in Chapter 7, we will talk about happy home practices that will encourage a happy home environment that your husband and your children will want to return to at the end of every hectic day.

Part III : Family

Second, we will discuss family relationships. Families are an interesting societal structure. Think about it. Friendships are usually between two people and are based on their shared interests. Business relationships often have someone at the top who delegates workloads to managers, who then delegate workloads to those beneath them.

Families are not like this! Mom and dad are equal partners with VERY different responsibilities. We will talk about how these responsibilities work together and what that means for your children. Most importantly, I will help you find a balance between your role as a wife and your role as a mother.

Family unity will be one of the first things we cover, in Chapter 8, because I believe that it is often overlooked. Chapter 9 will then talk about your relationship with your husband and follow it up with a discussion on your children in Chapter 10. Lastly, in Chapter 11, we will touch on extended family and friends (more or less, the world outside your home.)

Part IV : Self

Lastly, we will discuss your sense of self. This piece of information is so important to me. How can we balance motherhood and individualism? That is a REALLY hard question to answer because as mothers we are being pulled in about 30 different directions at any given moment.

When I was first married, I did not feel that I had lost my sense of self much at all. I taught dance classes, music lessons, and worked hard on building a business. I had a lot of projects that I was really invested in for myself and not for anyone else.

STORY TIME: I got pregnant with my daughter about four months into marriage and immediately got really sick. Because of this I ended up quitting all of my jobs, and ending all of my personal projects. Eventually my daughter was born, and I was feeling better. I wasn't sick, I had a wonderful husband who showed me immense support, and I had a beautiful little girl who I loved and cherished. Over time, though, I realized that all of my time was spent supporting my husband and daughter, as I had given up all personal goals during my pregnancy. This is NOT a bad thing, but it can make one a little wary that they are making no personal progress in their life. That is when I went on a major search to find ways to work on my sense of self, without ignoring my family and their needs.

We're going to cover, in Chapter 12, the best ways to foster a supportive environment for personal growth in your home. Chapter 13 will specifically touch on my "Power Hour" technique, that will help you (and your husband) support each other in personal endeavors. Lastly, Chapter 14 will discuss how to balance your wellness in the 8 elements with your responsibilities to your family and home.

Types of Imbalance

Home, Family, and Self are three points in a mother's triangle of happiness. To make the triangle whole, you need all three points to be present. A lot of times, we negate the importance of one aspect of our responsibilities because we would rather spend our time doing something else.

You can think of mothers that you have known in your lifetime that latch onto one or two aspects and neglect the other(s). I like to call these next few examples the "Mommy Personalities." When reading through these examples, you may find a personality type that sounds like you. Know that these are fluid personalities. You are not stuck in one, and you will not have only one personality type for your whole life. You are an individual and the beautiful thing about that is that you have free agency to change and improve.

No Point: This mother does not pay any mind to home, family, or self.

Miss Meltdown

We will start with the mother that struggles the most. Miss Meltdown cannot seem to get her life together in any aspect. This is not always the fault of the mother. Sometimes it is due to mental illness, sometimes it is due to alcohol, drugs, or some other addiction, and sometimes the mother just does not care about anything. This is the far end of the spectrum. Most mothers do not fit into this category, and the ones that do are generally in need of intervention. This mother should never feel afraid to reach out to others, amidst their struggles, to help them get back on their feet.

Single Point: This mother often "overachieves" in one aspect to a fault.

Miss OCD

This mother is solely focused on home. On the outside, it may look like she has everything under control; however, often she takes no time for herself and no time for her family because she is focused on outward appearances. This mother can also sometimes come across as a drill sergeant. Her home is spotless, beautiful, and organized, but often at the expense of her relationships and her health.

Miss Selfish Slob

This mother is solely focused on herself. She will neglect to care for her home and neglect her family to engage in activities that make her happy. She may indulge in expensive purchases for herself or leave the kids with dad often to have time to do the things she wants to do. She does not seek out her family's approval but instead looks to outsiders for praise.

Miss Deluded

This mother is solely focused on family, but to an unhealthy extent. Often this woman is not very confident, and instead of running her household she will allow her children (and sometimes husband) to walk all over her. She may be prone to buying them anything they want to seek their approval or love. She will cave to her family members' whims in hopes that it will make them happy.

Double Points: This mother is fairly balanced, but lacking in one aspect.

Miss 'Me' Mom

This mother is a little more well-rounded. She takes care of her home and herself. Unfortunately, she will neglect her relationship with her husband and her children. A clean home helps her keep up good appearances, and she makes sure to take care of herself and her needs. This can leave the family resentful towards her.

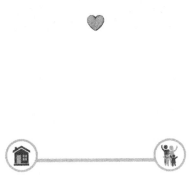

Miss Selfless to a Fault

This mother also has more bases covered. She takes care of her home and family. Often times she will neglect her own well-being for the sake of others. This mother is intent on keeping her home in order and making sure her relationships in her family are strong. Unfortunately, this can leave her feeling unaccomplished as an individual.

Miss Hot Mess

Like the "'Me' Mom" and "Selfless to a Fault Mom," Miss Hot Mess is trying pretty hard in most cases. She takes care of her family and herself. This means her relationships are strong with her family, and she is personally well-balanced, but she is all over the place at home! She constantly misses appointments, meals are all over the place, and the house is regularly messy.

Triple Points: This mother is completely balanced, and has mastered motherhood.

Miss Mother

This is the personality type we are aiming for. Miss Mother has learned to balance each facet of her life. Not only has this balance benefited her family and her home life, but it has also benefited her. She has become less stressed, deepened relationships with her husband and children, and adopted meaningful projects for herself.

This mother is NOT perfect, but she strives every day to make a difference in her home, family, and herself. That is what matters most: striving to be better and making baby steps to improve. Not being perfect from the get-go. As we all know, nobody is perfect!

Helpful Hint

For each chapter in this book, I suggest that you sit down with your spouse and discuss the things you have learned. This way, you and your spouse are on the same page. DO NOT sit him down and say, "My book says we have to…" because bashing my book over his head will make very little difference to him. Say something more along the lines of, "I feel like I am learning a lot from this book and it is really making me think about… How do you think we should apply these principles I have learned?" Then you can let the discussion build from there!

THE HOMEMAKING HANDBOOK

REFLECTION QUESTIONS

How well, on a scale from 1 to 10, do you feel you have mastered your home responsibilities?

How well, on a scale from 1 to 10, do you feel you have mastered your family responsibilities?

How well, on a scale from 1 to 10, do you feel you have mastered your responsibilities to your self?

If you could guess which "Mother Personality" fits you best, which would it be?

Which category of motherhood do you feel you excel at?
Home, Family, or Self?

Which category of motherhood will be a challenge for you?

50

PART 2 : HOME

52

5 : ORDER AND ORGANIZATION

Think of order and organization as the foundation of your home; from there you can build up, but without a working schedule, organized house, and budgeted finances you are not going to have the time, space, or money to invest in your family or yourself. Order and organization are probably your top priority as a mother. Scratch that. They are definitely your top priority. Although we will discuss them specifically in relation to your home, order and organization can also be applied to family and self.

Recently I have noticed a collection of articles that insist that messy people are real intellectual geniuses. The implication is that it is great if you are a messy person because that means you are smart, and not just smart, but you also have a creative, intelligent mind. While this may be true, there have also been links found between intelligence and mental illness.

Think about Van Gogh. He was extremely talented and creative, some would consider him a genius, but he also willingly chopped off his ear and mailed it to a woman he was in love with. He was also a mess. To summarize, being a mess isn't scientifically proven to be a benefit to anyone, and at least in my experience, there is a better way!

If you think about any successful business there is a great amount of order to it. There are working pieces that all speak to each other and work between each other to make the big business around them function. Bad businesses often lack an obvious structure, very few people know what is actually required of them, and eventually, the business's success dwindles.

This idea of order can and should be applied to our homes. Of course, we are not running a military camp, but building a foundation of order makes time, space, and money open up for the important things in our lives.

Cleaning

Cleaning is probably my least favorite aspect of motherhood; however, it might be the one area I am best at. I might not be a fan of cleaning, but I sure am a fan of a clean house! If you are looking for a few tips to make the cleaning go by faster and more enjoyably consider these ideas:

- Make sure to delegate chores!
- Know your daily, weekly, and yearly chore requirements.
- Play music while you clean.

Chore delegation is so important. Remember, you are a mother, not a maid. Cleaning up after everyone is not your job, but it is your job to facilitate how the work gets done. We will delve deeper into this in chapter 10, but for now, know that creating a chore system in your home will be a HUGE benefit to you.

All of your children's chores should be age appropriate. Your children should have daily chores that are simply required because they are a part of the household. This teaches your children that when everyone puts work into the home, the whole family benefits.

Mom's most important job, other than overseeing the delegation of chores, is knowing which chores need to get done. Lucky for you, in the free downloadable packet offered in the first few pages of this book, there is a printable weekly cleaning chart and yearly maintenance checklist that should give you the basics of what needs to get done.

First, consider chores that need to get done daily. This could include making beds, wiping down bathroom counters, emptying and loading the dishwasher, running a load of laundry, and taking out the trash. Once you have decided which chores are your family's daily chores, break them up into morning and night chores.

Next, I want you to consider things that should be done every week. I like to take each day of the week and assign a specific room in my house to that day. For example, Monday is focused on the living room. I make sure that room gets tidied, the furniture gets dusted, the floor is vacuumed, and the windows are washed. On Tuesdays, I move on to the bathrooms, then Wednesdays are bedroom days, and so on and so forth. This practice ensures that each room in the house gets special attention every week.

Lastly, we consider the yearly maintenance work that needs to be done. These are the big jobs that we often ignore until they are so gross that they cannot be ignored anymore. Think: vacuuming between cushions in the couch, dusting fans and lights, cleaning and changing filters, deep cleaning small appliances, cleaning out our food, and more. My free printable has a full checklist made just for you that is broken up by months. This can help you break up the workload over time. There are even spots to insert your own yearly maintenance work specific to your family.

We will discuss delegation and chore chart techniques in the "Children" chapter (chapter 10) to help you delve deeper into your cleaning plans. Remember that you and your family contribute to the same mess. Community mess = community responsibilities.

Scheduling

Guess what? You have already started scheduling your life! In just the last section, you decided which chores are morning chores, and which are night chores. All you have to do is set aside a set amount of time in the morning, and a set amount of time at night.

What are some other things we need to schedule for? Well, we are going to approach this the same way we approached cleaning. You are going to have a general daily schedule, a general weekly schedule, and then monthly activities. Pages 19-21 in the packet will help you immensely through this process!

Let's start by looking at your daily calendar. You will want to include what time the alarm goes off for everyone in the morning, meal times, school time, when you exercise, and a power hour. We will discuss this power hour more in a later chapter, but for now, just make sure to schedule in your power hour when you are either alone, or your husband is home to help with the kids. Think of any other daily needs, and make sure to schedule them in!

We move onto weekly schedules next. This will show what days the kids are in school, what days the kids' extracurricular activities are scheduled, and any other weekly appointments that apply. This could be church, book club meetings, piano lessons, Cub Scouts, and similar activities.

Lastly, you will want to take a look at your month. This should be done before the first day of every month as a family. We will discuss the details of this in the "Family Unity" chapter (chapter 8), but for now know that the monthly activities will play a relatively important part in your schedule.

Budgeting

The last section of order and organization we will cover is budgeting. We have already freed up our time through scheduling, and our space through cleaning, but now we need to make sure our money is being used in the best ways. This NEEDS to be done, at least to an extent, with your husband.

I will be up front and insist that if you are looking for a budget plan to give you the most freedom, you should read "The Total Money Makeover" by Dave Ramsey. I have also included a document on page 28 in the free workbook to help you run a budget meeting with your spouse BEFORE the first of every month.

First, you will consider your expenses. These are your monthly bills.

- Rent/Mortgage
- Utilities
- Phone Bill
- Health Insurance
- Car Insurance
- Car payment

Your monthly expenses will differ based on your family's needs but try to organize these in order from most important to least important.

Next, you will consider the fluid payments. These are costs that exist but are not set in stone. You want to decide your max budget for this item which means you will ALWAYS spend less than that amount.

- Groceries
- Clothing
- Date nights
- Gas
- Entertainment
- Babysitters

Like I said before, these amounts and items will be different depending on your family. Next, you will list debts. I strongly suggest applying Dave Ramsey's snowball method when paying off your debts.

- Student Loans
- Credit Card Debt
- Medical debts
- Home mortgage
- Car loan

Lastly, make sure you are putting money into a savings account every month!

We have a tendency to spend money we do not have, especially when we do not have an organized budget. When we organize a budget we often find that (a) we have less money than we thought or (b) we have way more money than we thought, but it is going to all the wrong places. Do not get stuck in either of these traps!

ALINA LAUREN

ACTION PLAN

☐ Assess how your space, time, and money are currently being allocated.

SPACE

☐ Make a list of daily chores. Break them up into morning chores and night chores.

☐ Make a list of weekly chores. Decide how these chores will be allocated.

☐ Make a list of yearly maintenance needs. Decide how these will be covered.

TIME

☐ Create a daily schedule for your family.

☐ Create a weekly schedule for your family.

☐ Set up a calendar for next month that can be seen by everyone in the household.

MONEY

☐ Set up a monthly budget meeting with your spouse. Sit down and make a budget today.

6 : HEALTH

Now that you've built a foundation of order and organization in your life in the most basic of ways, I'm going to introduce more elements of your life that you will need to fit in. I want to make something very clear: by the end of this book, you should have no "empty space" in your schedule. That means that every minute, hour, day, etc. is accounted for. **Empty time is wasted time.**

This doesn't mean that every hour of every day will be filled to the brim with work. In fact, I want you to consider the opposite. If you and your husband need to relax with a show at least once a day, schedule in that 45 minutes to an hour so that you can enjoy your show.

The problem happens when we fail to schedule in activities and we are left with a 4-hour binge-watching window that leaves us feeling lazy, useless, and unproductive. Sometimes lazy days happen. That is real life, believe it or not, and sometimes that is A-Okay. But lazy days that happen regularly can become toxic and pull you and your family out of these great habits that you are working to establish!

So now we are going to organize a plan for your health and your family's health. This includes actionable steps to organize a workout schedule, manageable meal plans, and remembering the little things that often go by the wayside.

Exercise

Exercise is simply your opportunity to find a way to be physically fit. I prefer lifting weights to running, but your plans may be completely different, and that's okay! It is simply important to stay active. This goes for you, your husband, and your children.

If it is easier, make a plan with your husband to work out together for 30 minutes to an hour every day. Maybe your husband prefers the gym, but you would rather just take the baby in the stroller early in the morning and get in a run. This will be something you decide.

Do not forget about the importance of your children's physical activity. Some of our children will participate in sports, sometimes we are blessed with a large backyard that they spend the afternoons exploring, but no matter HOW they are getting their exercise, it needs to be on the agenda.

This does not have to be a daily task. This can be a Monday, Wednesday, Friday task for now. Maybe, over time, you can work up to even more! The trick is that you need to find a way to make it work for you and your family.

It is good to remember that you can work on your physical health through strength training, endurance exercises, balance exercises, and stretching for flexibility. Maybe consider changing up your workouts every once in a while, just to stay well-rounded and let your body learn new techniques.

Meal Planning

Going into marriage and becoming the family cook was the scariest thing for me! I did not cook. I could follow recipes, but I had just never spent much time in the kitchen before getting married. Our meal experiences have definitely been rounds of trial and error, but I have found some good recipes and meal planning practices along the way.

These practices have saved me a lot of time, and a lot of money. Let's jump in and discuss the Meal Calendar first. This will become the centerpiece of your kitchen. It will be a reference for you as you journey to an organized life.

I suggest, right off the bat, that you purchase a whiteboard calendar and some different colored markers. I plan my meals for at least two weeks in advance, if not longer. This saves me time because I have to make fewer grocery trips. This also saves me money because I know exactly the food I need to purchase for the next two weeks.

Step one is to figure out your breakfast plan. I like to keep a round of three main breakfast meals that I filter through, then once a week we have a "gourmet" breakfast. It would look something like this:

			Two Week Plan			
SUN	MON	TUES	WED	THUR	FRI	SAT
Eggs	Shake	Oatmeal	Eggs	Shake	Oatmeal	Waffles
Eggs	Shake	Oatmeal	Eggs	Shake	Oatmeal	Waffles

This way, I buy far less in a variety of ingredients and I filter through ingredients quick enough that nothing is wasted. You will pick a colored marker to represent Breakfast, and write in each of your breakfast plans for the next (at least) 2 weeks. This is also great if you assign meal-making assignments to each of your kids. They know what is on the menu each day, so it is easy for them to help out.

Next, we make the same approach to lunches. I tend to use more variety with my lunches because I have more time to prepare them. I also homeschool so everyone is at home and I do not have to pack lunches. Depending on your lifestyle, your lunch plans will be different.

Once again, pick a colored marker to represent Lunch and write in your lunch plans for the next (at least) 2 weeks. When you are done, your calendar should include your breakfast and lunch plans for every day of the next two weeks.

Two Week Plan

SUN	MON	TUES	WED	THUR	FRI	SAT
Eggs P.B&J	Shake Quesadilla	Oatmeal Macaroni	Eggs P.B&J	Shake Quesadilla	Oatmeal Macaroni	Waffles Burritos
Eggs P.B&J	Shake Quesadilla	Oatmeal Macaroni	Eggs P.B&J	Shake Quesadilla	Oatmeal Macaroni	Waffles Burritos

Lastly, let's cover dinner plans. I tend to pick seven different meals and repeat the meals over the course of the two weeks. Pick simple meals for busy days, and more difficult meals for days where you have more time. Do not undervalue the usefulness of a crockpot. Afternoons and evenings can get hectic, especially if your children are in after-school programs, and having your meal cooking all day can make a real difference.

This is what your calendar should look like when you are finished:

Two Week Plan

SUN	MON	TUES	WED	THUR	FRI	SAT
Eggs P.B&J Pasta	Shake Quesadilla Fish Tacos	Oatmeal Macaroni Soup	Eggs P.B&J Casserole	Shake Quesadilla Salad	Oatmeal Macaroni Burgers	Waffles Burritos Pizza
Eggs P.B&J Pasta	Shake Quesadilla Fish Tacos	Oatmeal Macaroni Soup	Eggs P.B&J Casserole	Shake Quesadilla Salad	Oatmeal Macaroni Burgers	Waffles Burritos Pizza

The last considerations you will want to make are for snacks and desserts. I make maybe one dessert a week. I do not love baking, and I am not keen on standing around in our uncomfortable, tiny kitchen. Maybe someday that will change, but for now a batch of cookies once a week is good enough.

If you love baking bread then make sure to schedule in your baking days! Do you love canning? Put it on your list of things to schedule and plan for. Any food items that are making their way in and out of your kitchen need to be considered, but hopefully, this practice will help you cut down on the unhealthy purchases that you grab while walking down the aisles.

Now it is time to make yourself a grocery list. I like to keep cards of all of my recipes in a little recipe box. When I know the recipes I will be using for the next two weeks I pick them out of my box and go through each recipe one-by-one while checking to see what ingredients I have, and what ingredients I need. I proceed to fill in a list of all the things I need.

Now I want to move on to grocery shopping. As a mother, I've found that grocery shopping without my husband can be really frustrating. If your local grocery store has Free Pickup then I would 100% take advantage of it. This has been a lifesaver for me. Instead of wandering aisles for an hour or more every time I head to the grocery store, I grab my grocery list, shop online, order everything I need (find the cheap deals) and then pick up my groceries when they are ready for me.

If you choose to order online, you will need to schedule in time one day for ordering all of your groceries, then schedule in a pickup time the next day. The beautiful thing is that you can load your kids in the car, drive to get your groceries, keep everyone in the car while your groceries are being loaded in, then drive home. This saves you time and saves you money.

There should be one day every week, or every two weeks that you set aside for your grocery shopping expeditions. Sometimes you will actually need to walk in the store. Sometimes kids have grown out of their clothes, or you need to find specific items that were not available online.

Nutrition

Let's talk about general nutrition. Now you know how to set up a meal plan, but remember to keep your meal choices healthy and well-rounded. I am not a nutrition expert, and I will not pretend to be for the purposes of this book, but it is your responsibility as a mother to research and find the healthiest practices for your family.

Some families have to live gluten-free, others are catering to family members with lactose-intolerance. Some families have growing boys who eat a lot, and others have babies who require certain nutritional needs. This aspect of your health will be specific to you and your family. It may take some trial and error, but keep pushing!

An important aspect of health is water intake. If this helps your organizational skills, I would suggest you purchase a different colored water bottle for each child and encourage them to drink x-amount of water every day.

Helpful Hint

Speaking of color-coordinating: a great way to keep the kitchen clean is to make sure each child has a different set of plates, bowls, utensils, and cups catered to them. Color coding is a great way to do this, and that way you always know who left their mess at the table. You can implement this idea to school supplies and more.

Lastly, you should consider vitamins. For some families this will be unnecessary, for others, it will need to be part of the family's morning routine. Your vitamins may be different from person to person, but you need a clear schedule to follow.

Gardening

As discussed before in the meal planning section, sometimes we want to do things just for us. This can include baking bread, canning food, or even gardening. That's right! What better way to make sure you are getting healthy, nutritional produce than by growing it yourself.

Include your kids in the process so that they can learn, grow, and work. Depending on where you live you will only have so many options, but herb gardens take up a small amount of space and yield tasty results. You can also grow fruit trees, vegetable gardens, and more. This is obviously a personal preference situation, but it can save you money on groceries in the long run, and you can always have fresh produce at your disposal.

Depending on how far you go with your gardening and homesteading, you could also make a business of it and sell excess fruits, veggies, and more to your neighbors. A good investment could include chickens as well!

Hygiene

Lastly, let's consider basic hygiene practices that should be adhered to by every member of the family.

First, let's talk showers. Baths and showers tend to be part of the nightly routine. Make sure your kids recognize that a shower is part of their routine and not just an "I'm covered in mud and mom doesn't want it all over the house" situation. My husband and I differ on the shower front. He enjoys taking showers first thing in the morning and I enjoy taking showers right before I go to bed. It works out because I can cover my daughter's morning routine with ease, and she can get her quality time with dad right before bed.

Second, everyone needs to be brushing their teeth! Good tooth brushing habits will save on dental visits in the long run. Not only will your family save their teeth, but they will also save your budget! This is also a part of your child's routine. They should not be paid commission for fulfilling this chore.

Last, but certainly not least, there needs to be a strict bedtime. Sure, weekends can be a little more lenient, but if your children (or you and your husband) are lacking sleep, the schedule for the day can go way downhill really fast. There should be an alarm clock wake up in the morning for everyone, and a relatively strict bedtime, especially for the younger kids.

THE HOMEMAKING HANDBOOK

ACTION PLAN

- ☐ Put exercise time for you, your children, and you husband in the schedule.
- ☐ Plan your breakfasts, lunches, and dinners for the next two weeks.
    - o Make a grocery list based off of your meal plan.
    - o Add any dessert and snack ingredients you will need.
- ☐ Consider compiling all of your recipes onto recipe cards and keeping them in a recipe box.
- ☐ Schedule in two hours for meal planning.
- ☐ Schedule in grocery pickup days.
- ☐ Consider buying separate water bottles for each family member.
- ☐ Consider color-coding kitchen utensils.
- ☐ Make sure to write in times for family members to take their vitamins in your schedule.
- ☐ Would you like to bake your own bread, keep your own garden, or raise chickens? Consider your options and schedule in time for these activities.
- ☐ Plan morning and nighttime routines for your family.

7 : HAPPY HOME

So far, we have discussed the necessary elements of running a home so everything does not fall apart. Meeting physical necessities ensures that your home is livable, and your family stays alive. This chapter is less about physical needs and more about spiritual and emotional needs being met.

Our home is our castle. We need to treat it as such. That means more than just keeping it clean and keeping food on the table. We are a family after all.

I want to start off by touching on the "open door / closed door" policy. Your children need to understand that sometimes the door is open for friends to come over, and sometimes the doors are closed because you need family time.

When I was a teenager, I remember visiting a friend. They had an "always open door" policy, so there were always people there. I remember spending time with her up in her room then heading down to the kitchen to grab a snack with her. On the way down the stairs, her mother blew up. No, she did not explode and catch fire, but that may have been a lot less awkward because I would have known to make my way out of the house immediately. Instead, I was stuck sitting on the stairs for about 20–30 minutes just praying that the anger and yelling would end.

There are certain family matters that need to be kept within the family, if not for our own family members' sake, then for their friends' sakes. Some of these things include disciplining our children or simply spending the time to grow closer.

As a mother, it is your responsibility (along with your husband) to make these decisions. Maybe the time between dinner and bedtime is a closed-door window where chores are finished, bedtime routines are done, and family time is essential.

Beyond simply understanding that this unspoken rule should exist, what practices can we organize in our home to encourage a happy home? Let's explore.

Family Night

It is my firm belief that at least one night a week should be set aside for family. You can decide how you will apply this to your family, but I will give you an example. My family always makes sure there is an activity, mini-lesson, and treat involved. (This is generally the only day of the week that I make a dessert.)

As your kids get older, you can encourage them to take part in the family night by being in charge of treats or the activity. You can even add other elements to the night such as singing a song together, and more.

The important part is that your family makes an effort to spend quality time together. I encourage you to hold these family gatherings at your home so that the happy memories can be tied to the family instead of the movie theater or bowling alley. It is great to get out of the house and participate in activities as a family, but family night should be focused on the family instead of the activity. Board games are a great example of family activities.

As for the mini-lesson, this can be a religious lesson, a manner-based lesson, or a school-based lesson. It will depend on your family dynamic, but it should be a small lesson, 5–10 minutes. If you notice your children are having trouble sharing their toys you can discuss sharing for 5–10 minutes. If one of your kids is learning about something at school, you can take what they are learning and adapt it so that everyone learns something new. This will encourage a love of learning in the home.

Which leads us to our next subject…

Activity Stations

Activity stations for most families will apply to the young children. There are two parts to this practice, but for me, it applies to everyone in the family. Since I homeschool, "school" time is designated for our well-rounded activities. My young ones have very basic requirements for what they need to finish, and as the kids get older the requirements get a little more strict.

Let's start with a list.

The first thing you want to do is decide what kind of well-rounded activities you want your children to work on every day. My list looks a little like this:

- Reading
- Educational Show
- French
- Outside time
- Art
- Piano

This list will look different for each age group. If you are homeschooling then the list will be longer. If your kids spend a lot of their day at school then their list may only include after-school requirements such as:

- Practice piano
- Homework
- Free reading

It is likely that a lot of their art, P.E., and educational material will be covered in school. If you homeschool your children then your list will likely be a little bit longer. This is because their academic requirements are included in the list:

- Math
- Science
- Language Arts
- History
- Art
- P.E.
- French
- Music
- Educational Show

Each family's expectations will be different, but I suggest writing these out in a list format.

Applying the List

There are a couple of ways you can apply your lists. You can either create a separate schedule for each kid so that they know exactly what they need to be doing at what time, or you can set aside "activity time," and let your kids know that during that time they need to complete their checklist.

Do Good

I believe that our society has become a people of self-indulgence, with little regard for the people around them, and even less regard for how their time is used. In my life, I have learned to adopt my own little saying to keep my priorities straight, and I think it is a good mantra to encourage your children to learn and understand the implications of.

If it doesn't DO GOOD, what good is it?

Recently, weed was made legal in my home state. I was seeing blog post after blog post explaining why no one should care if others are smoking weed. The main argument is that "it wasn't hurting anyone." That's fine. It might not be hurting anyone, but who is it helping?

If your son plays video games alone for five hours every day, is he hurting anyone? No, but who is he helping? Is he even helping himself?

As a family, you need to decide what time spent on electronics is the appropriate time spent. There are a lot of decisions you will need to make that are not necessarily between good and evil. When you are faced with these decisions ask yourself, "Is this DOING GOOD?" If it is not, then, "What good is it? Really?"

THE HOMEMAKING HANDBOOK

ACTION PLAN

☐ Discuss the open door / closed door policy with your spouse. Make a clear decision on when friends are welcome and when family time is essential.

☐ Decide what night each week should be family night. Set aside that time in your schedule.

☐ Make lists for each family member that include well-rounded activities they should be covering every day.

☐ Set aside "activity time" in everyone's schedule.

☐ Discuss with your spouse activities that are prominent in your home that are not "doing good." Decide if and how these activities will fit into your schedule in the future.

80

PART 3 : FAMILY

82

8 : FAMILY UNITY

Are you ready to jump into something a little bit different? In my experience, most books for mothers are really good at covering requirements for scheduling and organization, but very few delve into your actual family relationships and how to build your family up as a unit.

This aspect of being a mother is so essential! So why is it set aside so often? I knew for the purposes of this book it NEEDED to be included. If your home runs smoothly, but your kids despise you and your husband is not excited about coming home from work then you have got a serious problem on your hands!

Although a lot of how your family members feel will be directly related to how we interact with them, we can go through some practices that will help your attitude, your husband's attitude, and your children's attitudes improve.

Your home should be a place where each family member feels

supported by everyone else. Dad should feel like his wife and children support him and appreciate his hard work to bring in an income that takes care of everyone. Mom should know that she is appreciated for all of the hard work she does to keep the household running smoothly, keep yummy meals on the table, and keep everyone healthy and happy. The kids should each know that their parents and siblings support them in their talents and that they love them for who they are. These roles may be different, depending on your family, but the support for each family member's role should be the same.

This is hard for any family because you have so many different personalities coming together to make one family work. My parents mastered the art of sustaining a supportive environment. We had three kids in our family: me and my two younger brothers. I was the artsy one. My mom made sure the family always attended my performances and competitions so each family member had an opportunity to show their support for my hard work. My younger brother loved soccer and later delved into rugby. Our family was at every game to support him. My youngest brother was interested in computers and loved messing with them. What did my parents do? They supported him in building his own computer that is, to this day, still the best running computer in my parent's home.

Though none of us shared any interests, I love watching soccer and rugby, and I call my brother regularly to talk about computers. This pattern of simply showing support has brought me and my siblings closer together. So, let's talk about how you can implement some steps to bring your family closer together.

Family Purpose

Have you ever been part of a company that did not have a mission statement or a vision? Probably not. Companies without some sort of vision very rarely last long. Every successful business needs a vision or a plan to make progress; otherwise, what are they working towards?

Oftentimes, individuals recognize that if this practice works for a business, it can work for them too. They make goals, set up a plan, and put the plan into practice so that they can see some success.

Why then, if individuals and businesses have figured out that this practice yields results have families not implemented the same strategies? We're going to jump right in and get started.

Creating a Vision

It's time for you to create a vision for your family and start setting goals. To do this, you will organize your goals and values into the eight elements we discussed before. This will help you more fully get a picture of your goals. We will first apply this concept to your family as a whole. Here are some examples:

Physical

Have more time to participate in extracurriculars and keep up a healthy active lifestyle

Learn proper eating habits and gardening skills

Encourage good hygiene habits in our home

Exercise every day

Eat fresh veggies every day

Learn to grow fruit trees

Emotional

Have a happy childhood, free from bullying

Learn to discuss our feelings with each other instead of yelling, slamming doors, and throwing tantrums

Work on not picking on our siblings

Intellectual

Children will maintain As and Bs in school

Each child will read a new book or novel every 2 weeks

Take a class outside of our comfort zone during every unit

Social

Spend more time with family

Invite friends over for activities

Plan a fun social event once a month

Write letters to extended family on Sundays

Occupational

Start working towards a vocational goal

Build up a vocational skill

Start a home business: crafting, yard work, etc.

Environmental

Establish a safe environment to learn in

Set up a chore chart/board and follow through

Keep our rooms clean and tidy

Always pick up toys immediately after playing with them

Spiritual

Participate in a large service project every month

Attend church regularly

Do service for our neighbors

Financial

Provide opportunities to prepare financially for the future

Offer children a commission based on their willingness to work

Give 10% and save 40% of our income

These are simply examples and not all are necessary for your family. As parents, we should come up with goals that match the family's best interests, and we can always include some input from the kids. Print these goals and place them somewhere where you will see them regularly and be reminded.

Now you can repeat this process, but with each child individually. This will help each of your family members develop their own individual goals and plans.

Family Dinners

Families need to have time together every day to bond. A really great way to do this is to make sure family dinners happen daily. For some families, this will be difficult because of work hours or miscellaneous extracurricular activities that are only offered at night and during dinner time.

Maybe, for your situation, a family breakfast will be more of a possibility. No matter when it occurs, there should be a designated meal for family bonding. What better way to bond than over food?

Family Councils

Every once in a while, we need to reassess where our family is at, how we can improve, and what actions need to be implemented. It is my firm belief that there should be 4 separate family councils every month.

- Family
- Couple
- Couple with Kids
- Parent & Child

The Family Council

This council should include the whole family and a calendar. Your main discussion will be the schedule for the month. Make sure that everyone's activities and appointments are organized on the calendar and that everyone knows what is going on throughout the month.

You can use this time to talk about achievements and encourage your kids to be aware of each other. This is a time to connect, strengthen, and solidify your relationships as a family.

Couple Council

This is a council only between you and your spouse. You can talk about each of your kids, changes you can make in your parenting to help them, and ways to manage sibling rivalries. This is also a great time to discuss your relationship with each other and how it can be improved. Remember to always come from a place of love!

Couple & Kids Council

This is a council between you as a couple and your individual kids. This is the perfect opportunity to learn about ways you can improve family relationships, learn about struggles your child is facing, and find ways to support your child in their personal endeavors.

Parent & Child Council

This is much like the previous council, except there will only be one parent involved. You can decide to do this in many different ways. You can have father/son and mother/daughter councils, you can make sure each child gets one-on-one time with each parent, or you could simply make sure the parent your child is most comfortable talking to gives them one-on-one attention.

This council is far less organized and may just be a passing moment between a parent and child. Sometimes in passing moments children will open up about struggles in their lives that they feel uncomfortable approaching their parents about in a structured manner. These situations should be shared later to the other spouse so that everyone is aware of the situation and can be supportive.

THE HOMEMAKING HANDBOOK

ACTION PLAN

☐ Organize times this month for the four different types of family councils.

☐ At your family councils, make sure to create family goals and individual goals that you and your family can start working towards. Use the eight elements as your guide.

9 : HUSBAND

I understand that not every family will be a nuclear family. For a variety of different reasons, a husband and father may not be present in your home structure. If that is the case, then you may decide to skip this chapter. Know that you need support, even if it does not come from your spouse. As a single mother, it can be very difficult and even impossible to manage everything alone. Don't forget to find resources to help make up for responsibilities that a spouse is not there to manage.

Work. Work. Work. Yes, marriage is fun, exciting, thrilling, and more, but it is also a lot of work. Work does not need to be frustrating. There are plenty of people who find enjoyment in their work. This is what we are striving for.

If you have a husband and father in the home, then there are some basics we should cover about your relationship. First of all, every marriage is going to be different. How you make your marriage work is between you and your husband. I will give you basic tips and tricks to making it work, but you and your husband can adjust based on your needs.

People Priorities

If I were to ask you to sit down and write a list of people in your life, in order of importance, I hope your husband would be at the top of this list. Your spouse should come first. Yes, there are situations where your children will need your immediate attention, but in general, your spouse should be your first priority. All of your kids will eventually move out and you and your husband will be left alone together. You do not want to save all of your connecting with your spouse and becoming one until after your kids move out. You want this to be a continuous process.

Remember that your relationship with your spouse is a partnership. You are equal but different. You, as a wife and mother, and your spouse, as a husband and father, are equal in value, but you will contribute complimentary traits to your marriage and family. If you both did exactly the same jobs and took care of the same responsibilities then there would be missing pieces all over your family life. You will give equally in different ways, but you are there to "serve" your children together. Your responsibility to your spouse comes first, then as a team, you take care of your kids.

Simply remembering this will make a huge difference in your family life! Remember to remind your children how important dad is to the family. Your young kids will not understand how their dad's hard work in his career transfers into the food on their table, the roof over their head, and the clothes on their skin.

Structure of Support

Our spouse should be our strongest supporter, and we should be the strongest supporter of our spouse. How can you support your husband? The best way to know the answer to this is to ask. Ask your husband. Start the conversation. "How can I support you?" Your spouse's answer will be completely different from my husband's! Sometimes, you do not even have to ask, you simply listen to the things they thank you for.

During law school, my husband was taking 18 credits during one semester. He was busy and exhausted on a regular basis. One day he came home, ate dinner, cuddled up with me on the couch, and thanked me for having dinner ready. He was so glad he could relax and enjoy my company and our daughter's company when he got home without having to worry about making food for himself.

From that moment, I knew I could show him support by making sure I had a meal ready for him at the end of the day. Did I always manage to accomplish this? Definitely not, but my husband also knew that those days were days when I needed his support.

Receiving support from our spouse may be more difficult in some situations. Sometimes we need to be patient with our spouse because we only have so much time, money, and resources at our disposal.

Take my husband's three years in law school as an example. A lot of my husband's focus was going primarily into building up a career so that in the long run he could support his family. This meant that for those three years I really had to step up my game at home. My husband was less capable of supporting me with specific needs, and I had to recognize the need for patience on my part in that situation.

Sometimes we feel support through receiving gifts from our partner, but we are lacking in funds. Sometimes support is time to spend on our own, but our spouse's schedules are filled to the brim.

You have two options: either you and your spouse consider changing your situation, or you acknowledge that the situation is temporary and find creative ways to make it work.

Responsibilities

What responsibilities does each spouse hold in your family? This will differ from family to family, but there are some basics that you can refer to.

Father's Responsibilities

Preside. Provide. Protect. These three Ps are a good guide for fathers. This list gives a father purpose. Often men feel like their only purpose is to provide money. This is changing more and more as women are seeking careers, but in a nuclear family this can be a very valid concern. Dad should not feel like he is only useful because of the income he brings to the family.

Presiding is to love, serve, and sacrifice. It does not include ruling over the family or being the boss. Of course, this responsibility is also part of your responsibilities. Presiding is not specific to your husband. You should both love, serve, and sacrifice for your family.

A husband and father should also provide. This may be based around his ability to work outside of the home, especially with young, nursing children at home. It is primarily the father's responsibility to make sure the family has an income that can cover their expenses. Situations and circumstances may change the possibility of this, but it is a general rule.

Protecting, lastly, is the primary role of the father. I like to make sure my husband understands this when big bugs have infiltrated our home. He's pretty talented when it comes to protecting me from bugs. Beyond physical protection, husbands can offer spiritual and emotional protection as well. This can come as kind and understanding responses to conflict in the home, and support for his wife and children in conflicts outside of the home. Maybe your spouse can offer guidance to your children to help protect them from outside influences that threaten their health, safety, and happiness.

Mother's Responsibilities

A mother's primary responsibility is to nurture. To nurture is to "care for and encourage the growth or development of." This mainly applies to our children but also applies to our relationship with our husband, and our treatment of ourselves. Women, through their natural nurturing abilities, can encourage growth, learning, and loving among their family members.

Although nurturing is the primary concern of the mother, running the home is a secondary responsibility. This is especially true if you are at home while your husband is at work. Remember, this does not mean you are the maid, it means you facilitate the workload required in running a household.

Variations

Obviously, this is a simplified version of a mom and dad's separate responsibilities. It is a basic blueprint for making sure the family and home run smoothly. There will be variations on this affected by your husband's ability to work, your decision to enter a career, or simply a need for more funds.

Even more factors will go into deciding who is in charge of what responsibilities, but remember that those decisions are solely between you and your spouse. The decisions you and your spouse make may only be temporary, but they may also be permanent. For example, while my husband was in law school, we decided it was my responsibility to be the primary breadwinner. Luckily, I was able to do this from home and still nurture my children, but it was an extra responsibility on my plate that we knew was a necessary, temporary situation.

Your life will always be changing, and you may always have to reconsider who holds what responsibilities, but keeping that line of communication open is most important.

ACTION PLAN

- [ ] Ask your husband, "How can I support you?" Take note of his answer, and make adjustments to your scheduling, planning, and behavior.
- [ ] Decide what responsibilities each spouse holds. Discuss whether these responsibilities are temporary or permanent.

ALINA LAUREN

10 : CHILDREN

Once we decide to start a family with our spouse, our children become the center of our lives. Suddenly everything revolves around them and their well-being. As a new mother, or even as an experienced mother, it is possible to feel that we are not quite meeting the needs of our children. We may worry that we are not making the right decisions for our kids.

Everyone feels this way at some point. Though there are hundreds of books on parenting, almost every book seems to have conflicting information on how to raise your children. This is because there is no "one way" to raise your kids. How you interact with a son will be different than how you interact with your daughter. Even daughter to daughter you would find that different parenting techniques work for each.

We will discuss a few aspects of the family that are important in helping your children grow. Although you will approach these situations differently, there are questions that you and your husband need to ask yourselves as you are making plans.

In the last chapter we discussed that your responsibility as a mother is primarily to nurture. Nurturing is defined as "caring for and encouraging the growth or development of." This chapter will help you discover healthy ways to nurture your children in understanding the value of hard work, experiencing a love of learning, and building on their talents.

Hard Work and Responsibility

As parents, we can drive our children and ourselves to learn hard work and responsibility. By the time you are a parent, you have had a lot of responsibility thrust onto you. Generally, getting to where you are at has also required a lot of hard work.

Life will naturally require hard work and responsibility from us, but how can we as parents help our kids get a head start on building these traits? The best way is to give them opportunities to work and to be responsible.

The beautiful thing about young children is that they are interested in EVERYTHING. If I pull out the vacuum then my daughter is on her feet ready to help me. Same with the broom. When I am cooking in the kitchen, my daughter wants her own bowls and spoons to help me cook.

In general, little kids want to be doing what Mom and Dad are doing. A lot of times we insist they should not help because they will not do it right. I encourage you to hesitate when you want to say no to a helping heart. Obviously, sometimes we have to say no for safety reasons. No, our child cannot help us get things out of the oven, but they can more or less help sweep the floor. It may take a few more minutes to finish, but their willingness to work hard and help will not be squashed.

I would like to introduce my Agency Policy. The Agency Policy basically states that children don't naturally carry all the negative associations with "work" that adults do. This is why there are a plethora of children's toys that mimic parent's "toys." There are cleaning supplies, kitchen sets, and more. Things that adults would consider "work" become toys and games in the minds of children. Therefore, if we implement the Agency Policy, we allow our children's free agency to lead their willingness to work and help.

Because of this, our language in the home will change from statements to questions. "Clean up your toys this instant," will become, "Will you help me by cleaning up your toys?" Children have more of a natural inclination to help, than an inclination to follow rules. Additionally, questions and requests have a kinder tone than rules and regulations.

It is important to note that the "Agency Policy" only works if you are leading your children by example. They will learn to mimic you. In fact, your children are your best copycats. They want to be just like you! Make sure you are the best example you can be.

Your kids will learn hard work best through chores. They need to be responsible for their fair share. Sometimes, it may seem like it is easier if you just do everything because it will get done the right way.

Sometimes the right way is not the best way. If we continue to do our child's work for them, they do not get practice learning to do it right. Their experience is the best way!

Then we come to the question of paying allowances. Should we pay a set allowance? For some families, this is a no-brainer. It may just not be in the budget. That's fine, but when it is possible in the budget, what do we do about it?

One of my top suggestions is that you NEVER pay an allowance, you pay a commission. An allowance is given whether earned or not. A commission is earned based on the work put in. The rest of your children's lives will be filled with earning something for the work they put forward. This is a great way for them to start learning how that works.

Your children will get older and eventually want to either get a job or start their own business. This could be as simple as a babysitting business or as difficult as creating an online shop. Do not do the work for them. Let them do it for themselves, but be there to support them. When your kids get to this point, teach them about the importance of saving up for big purchases. A college degree. A car. An expensive road trip. You name it.

School

All parents will have to deal with school in some form or another, so how do we handle it? Once again, it will be different for each child! We are going to primarily discuss this from a scheduling standpoint. I want to look at two different forms of schooling. Obviously, there are many variations of schooling, but I will use two examples.

Homeschooling

Homeschooling is a bit of my forte. In fact, most of my company is based around homeschooling. If you're looking for value-packed online courses, as well as printable resources, then check out our shop at https://prismperfect.com.

When it comes to scheduling for homeschooling you can do it in a number of ways. You can either schedule specific blocks of time for classes, or you can schedule when school begins and when it ends, then allow your children to get their work done in the order they feel comfortable.

There is no "right way" to schedule your homeschooling lifestyle; however, I strongly suggest you keep all of your school scheduling separate from your home life. Schooling has the tendency to put a lot of stress on everyone. It is important to remember to keep your school stress confined to those hours in the day. It would probably help if you printed a separate school schedule for each of your children so they know what they are doing and when they are doing it. This way you could set off an alarm at certain intervals and they know exactly what assignment they are moving on to.

Regular School

This is generally referring to public school, but includes charter schools, private schools, and magnet schools. These are basically the same but have some variations. In general, your schedule will include the time they leave for school and the time they return. Unlike with homeschooling, you will have a commute to schedule in.

It is likely that your children will almost always come home with homework. Depending on their grade level and the school they are attending the time you need to set aside for homework may cover a wide range of time. Each child will also have different expectations and thus their homework time after school will be different than their siblings'.

What is the best way to manage this? Give each of your kids a fluid schedule. This will look more like a list than a schedule. For example, your youngest child will get home around 3:20. They will likely want a snack. They will have homework to finish. They may also need to practice the piano, and be ready for soccer practice at around 5:30. Their schedule will look something like this.

3:20 p.m.	Arrive home and have a snack
	Practice Piano
	Work on Homework
5:15 p.m.	Leave for practice
6:30 p.m.	Dinner
	Finish any homework & chores
	Bedtime routine
9:00 p.m.	Bedtime

Their Dreams

Our children will have hopes and dreams as early as their first words escape their mouths. Their dreams will also change a lot over the course of their lives. This means that we as parents need to be aware of their ever-changing moods, passions, and interests.

By no means does this mean we sign our children up for three months of horseback riding lessons only to find out that two weeks in they really are not interested and they want to quit. We should teach our children to be finishers. This also does not mean that if they choose to start ballet at the age of three that we force them to continue ballet until they move out. There should be a happy in-between that you, your husband, and your children can figure out together.

Fortunately, public schools offer a decent amount of variety in learning which can help our children get a taste of new things. From there, your child can choose one or two interests to really focus on and perfect. I think that as a general rule, picking one instrument and one sport is a great idea.

Some children will have absolutely no interest in sports or music. I still think it is a good idea for them to get a basic understanding or ability in each. Often sports are a great way to socialize and participate in activities with others. A lot of research has been done into the positive effects of music education, but it can be especially useful if you are religious because it can come in handy when people are looking for a volunteer pianist or performer.

Besides encouraging your children to participate in quality extracurricular activities, you will have the job to support them. Of course, the whole family participates in supporting each other, but remember that mom and dad should be a child's biggest fans!

Lastly, if you are having trouble finding something that interests your child, you can go through a list of classes and sports that your local recreational center is offering and let your child pick a couple that sound interesting. This will give your child an opportunity to try new things.

THE HOMEMAKING HANDBOOK

ACTION PLAN

- ❏ Create a chore chart for your children.
- ❏ Decide if and how you will pay your child a commission for their work.
- ❏ Make sure to decide what types of jobs earn what types of rewards. Making your bed should simply be done every day; however, if your child washes the car alone, you may consider paying them.
- ❏ Plan school schedules for each of your children. This includes extracurricular activities and homework that needs to be finished after school.
- ❏ Help your children discover unique interests. Consider including a sport and a musical instrument.

11 : EXTENDED FAMILY AND FRIENDS

We are going to step out of your home for a minute and consider the relationships you hold with extended family and family friends. Even though they may not be an active part of your daily life they are surely a part of your life that cannot be ignored.

I understand that the family dynamics between in-laws will vary across the board. Each family is different, and your differences deserve attention. The things I am talking about in this book are here to make you think, and they should encourage you to create a plan for your family. And only your family.

I will discuss a few different things in this chapter, the first being, "What does it mean to cleave?" Then I will move on to talk about toxic relationships, and how we can handle them with grace. Lastly, I want to touch on the fun stuff which includes being involved with your extended family and friends and keeping those relationships flowing even as you keep a strong focus on your immediate family.

I want to include a note that the comments I make in this chapter are based on my own experience in improving my relationships. As I've made clear in the rest of the book, you will need to tailor these ideas and practices to yourself. I would very strongly encourage prayer and personal consideration, especially in such cases that involve your relationships with family and friends.

Cleave

Genesis 2:24 of the Bible states, "Therefore shall a man leave his father and his mother, and shall cleave unto his wife: and they shall be one flesh." Now you may or may not be religious, but I want to use this verse as a lesson. I believe the moment this refers to is the moment of marriage. This is a big moment for all parties involved! This is a moment where a man and a woman take that next big step toward filling their parents' shoes. They will do just as their parents did before them.

This is also a very difficult moment for everyone involved because now everyone has to learn how to make it work. You have two families to visit on the holidays. You have a whole new family dynamic of the children who are not children anymore. There is a lot for everyone to learn.

So, what does it mean to cleave to our spouse? To cleave to someone is to stay very close to someone. I like to think my husband and I are glued at the hip. If I am having a conversation with someone in my extended family or with a friend, I imagine my husband is right there by my side. If I feel tempted to say something about my husband that he would not approve of if he were standing there, then I decide I should probably zip my lips.

I believe that broken relationships can be caused by seeking help outside of the relationship instead of inside the relationship. In some cases, seeking help in the form of marriage counseling can be extremely beneficial for you and your spouse. I'm not denying the value of seeking help, especially with your spouse, to improve your relationship. In most cases, though, if you are having a difficult time with your spouse, it is better to tell them instead of telling your friends. Be clear and kind about what is bothering you and why it is bothering you, then find a way together to fix it.

I would encourage you to not to make your experiences in marriage a "book club" topic. For example, this could include sharing chapters and episodes in your life that include personal information or inappropriate amounts of information with those outside of your marriage. When you reach out to others for help, your intentions should always be to seek ways to improve your relationship, not to vent about your frustrations with your spouse. Often, instead of making you feel better about the situation, you will feel more rooted in your opinions of the situation, and that will make it even more difficult when you address the issue with your husband later. Heaven forbid you let slip that, "My mom thinks that if you really loved me then you would…" or something similar.

On a last note, do not think for a moment that your parents are all of a sudden obscure folk who cannot give good advice. Sometimes they can be great tools for you and your spouse! But that is the key. Seek out your parents together to ask for their input and advice in very specific situations. They can be an answer to your prayers.

Let Them Fade

Unfortunately, toxic relationships exist. There will be times when you may wonder how to proceed with a friend or family member that is way out of line.

This may be a sister who insists on showing up drunk at every family event. This could be a friend that does not understand boundaries with your husband. This could be a mother that calls to scream at you for five hours over a post on social media. This may even be an abusive spouse. There will be different levels of toxicity in the relationship, but you probably have at least one or two people in mind.

As painful as it is, generally it is not the best idea to ignore the situation and act like nothing is happening. We should hesitate to completely break ties and cut people off, especially when family is involved, but we also do not want to encourage bad behavior to grow into a toxic relationship that causes problems. In some extreme situations, completely cutting off relationships is necessary.

I have two tips that have helped me in dealing with situations like this.

1. Remember to love.

2. Make sure you are consistent in sharing and maintaining rules

and boundaries.

First, please do not stop loving this person and showing them your support in the good things they do. Everyone is capable of good things, so try to look past the bad and show support when you see the good. Show them that you do care.

Unfortunately, sometimes we want to show that we care about someone so much that we will unintentionally encourage bad behavior just so we do not hurt their feelings or make them angry. We should not go out of our way to tell them we think they are wrong; however, we should make it clear that, whatever the action is, it is not appropriate in our homes.

This leads me to the second point. Let's say you are hosting a party and you invite a friend or coworker who smokes. They decide to smoke a few cigarettes in your yard. If, for instance, you are not comfortable with anyone smoking in or near your house, you can request that they go somewhere else if they need to smoke. Hopefully, this person will understand and respect your rules, but if they do not then you may have to stop inviting them over.

In the end, it is a show of respect. You respect that they have certain personality traits that may not align with your beliefs. At the same time, they do need to respect you and your home in order to be invited there.

Party On

Inevitably there will be many family get-togethers or celebrations that we will want to invite our family to. Do it! Make sure your family knows that you support them on their birthdays, graduations, anniversaries, and more. Then make sure that you involve them in your celebrations.

This will be different family to family. Showing support can be something as simple as a text on a special day or dropping off a gift. It could also be something as extravagant as throwing a surprise party. Decide that every Sunday you will make an effort to call your parents. Plan on reaching out to your siblings once a week or once a month. Our connections to community and family are important. Do not let your relationships fall through the cracks.

If you are interested in a party planning printable, check out the free download!

THE HOMEMAKING HANDBOOK

ACTION PLAN

- ☐ Make a list of important relationships in your life and in your spouse's life.
- ☐ Go through your list and decide the best way to keep healthy relationships with each person.
- ☐ Talk with your spouse and decide how you and your family will spend holidays.

PART 4 : SELF

12 : PREFACE

We are jumping into the third and final factor of your motherhood responsibilities, and that is self! Home and family are two very important factors, but your personal health, growth, and happiness are just as important. Not more important, not less important.

As we delve into this section I want you to think of things that are important to you. Think about the eight elements we discussed earlier and consider some personal goals you may have in each. This could include getting in shape, starting a business, or learning to paint.

Your first step is to create general goals. The examples above are a good jumping off point. Look at each of the eight elements and come up with a general goal.

Example:

Physical - Get in shape

Emotional - Learn to bullet journal

Intellectual - Read more books

Social - Have extended family dinners on weekends

Occupational - Start an Etsy shop

Environmental - Redecorate the living room

Spiritual - Become closer to God

Financial - Save up an emergency fund

After you have come up with general goals pick a few to focus on before you add the others into your plan. Then you will want to pick them apart and decide on ways you can bring the goals to fruition. Let's take getting in shape and use it as an example.

Step One: Start by finding a long-term, specific goal.

"I will lose 25 pounds."

Step Two: Figure out what steps need to be taken to reach that point.

"First, I need to cut out sugary foods from my diet. Then, I need to make an exercise plan. Last, I need to purchase any necessary equipment."

You can apply these two steps to each general goal. "Save up an emergency fund," becomes "Save $1,000," which then transitions to, "Put $100 in the savings account every week until the balance reaches $1,000." "Read more books," becomes, "Read 24 novels this year," which becomes, "Read a novel every two weeks." You can then make a list of the novels you will be reading over the course of the year.

Breaking down our goals into baby steps helps us pursue them with purpose. You did not graduate high school by saying, "I will graduate high school." You broke that big goal down into baby steps. "I will finish my homework assignments every night, and study for tests on Fridays. I will also make sure to designate X-amount of time to projects."

You are probably thinking that it is great to have these goals and baby steps, but how do I make it happen? You can and you will! In the "Be Supported" section we will discuss all of the necessary changes you will have to make to get the tools you need, find time to focus and get the support from your family.

Self Focus > Selfishness

Yes, we are now delving into maintaining your sense of self and taking care of yourself. These things are important, but there are going to be plenty of times when you feel overwhelmed, stressed, or even neglected as a wife and mother. Even if that's uncomfortable, it's okay. It is a natural part of taking on these responsibilities.

My biggest encouragement here is to remind you that these moments are temporary and they will pass as you bring about this focus on finding balance. Remember that your focus on self is based on building your talents and improving your health. If your focus instead becomes self-indulgence then you'll need to take a few steps back and evaluate.

This is why creating these goals will be so important. Creating goals will give you a vision of future growth instead of simply scheduling in a "me" hour every day. As you focus on self-growth you will start to experience the healing that comes by creating that balance between your home, your family, and yourself. This focus, not self-indulgence, will be the key.

Work Your Family In

How do we work our family into our dreams? Think about ways that your family supports dad in pursuing his dreams. How does the family help each individual child pursue their dreams? There are generally two factors. Anyone who is pursuing a dream simply needs these two Ts. Time and Tools.

I am going to give you the example from my husband's life, then apply it to you. His big dream was to be able to support his family and earn a comfortable income so that we would never be in need. Law school was not his plan A, but it ended up becoming a part of the plan. How did we as a family support my husband through this law school journey to achieve his dream of being able to support his family?

First, we made sure my husband had all of the tools he needed to succeed. My husband's tuition was a top priority, as well as his textbooks and his new laptop. These tools were important to him succeeding in law school. We also made sure he had time. My husband spent hours a day at school, and to save him time, my daughter and I would take a walk in the afternoons to bring him a healthy, cheap lunch. I always made sure home was covered so that he had the time to focus on his studies.

These two Ts can be applied to your goals too! Maybe you have a dream to lose 15 pounds. Your husband and family can support you by making sure you have the tools you need; this could be exercise equipment, a gym membership, or exercise videos for you to use at home. Then your family can give you time to exercise every day. Maybe you would like to spend one hour a day to exercise, shower, and meal plan.

Let's look at another example. Maybe you are looking to start an Etsy shop selling home-crafted items. Your husband and family could support you by providing the tools you need to build your products, as well as the time to sit down and construct them.

Whatever your dreams are, discuss with your family the tools and time necessary to pursue this dream, then put it into practice.

Be Supported

Find ways for your family to support you, just as you support them. Besides time and tools, there is a 3rd T: Tribute. This is praise. Your husband should always feel that you support him. Are there ways that you show him your thanks for his hard work, and your praise for his accomplishments? If not, consider ways to do that now.

You could give tribute by simply saying, "Congratulations, you have achieved so much in _____, and I am very proud of you!" Sometimes we show praise by throwing a party for a major achievement; this could be graduating, receiving a promotion, or a mile marker in a project. There are many different ways to pay tribute to someone's hard work.

The point I am trying to make here is that we are constantly praising our children for their accomplishments, and hopefully we find ways to praise our husbands daily, but this practice needs to extend to you as a mother. Being a mother can be a thankless job, and it is important for the whole family to be aware of mom's achievements and to support her as well.

The third T can be organized at the family council. Everyone in the family can be aware of everyone else's projects and dreams that they are pursuing. As a family, you can help each other set goals, and once the goals are accomplished everyone can celebrate.

Dreams and goals pursued alone can become impossible to achieve because you have no one backing you up. You also have no one keeping you accountable for your deadlines and goals. This is why the third T is so important for us when seeking success.

Remember. Tools, Time, and Tribute. These three Ts will help you accomplish and achieve anything with the support of your family. These three Ts will also help your husband and children each achieve their own goals and ambitions. You should discuss these three Ts in family council together so that everyone is on the same page and ready to support their family members!

THE HOMEMAKING HANDBOOK

ACTION PLAN

☐ Discover your general goals. Turn your general goals into specific goals. Make a list of baby steps you will need to take to achieve your goals.

☐ Gather with your family. Have everyone bring their list of goals. Decide on the tools, time, and tribute necessary to accomplish each goal.

13 : THE POWER HOUR TECHNIQUE

Let's discuss time. Time is one of our most valuable assets, and we are each allotted the same amount of time every day. How we use this time will determine what we can achieve. How we use this time will also determine how much money we make, or how much progress we can make in a project.

This is what helped me to create the Power Hour technique that I use daily in my own life. It will take time to see the results of this technique because it requires a lot of discipline. I have learned that it is not about how much time we have in a day to designate to a project, but what we do with the time we are given.

There are people who can work for hours on a project that someone else can finish in minutes. This can be due to their experience in whatever the project is, but it can also be due to their work ethic and the ability to focus and work fast.

Some things will simply need to just take time. When you want to get in better shape, you simply need to put in the work and wait for the results. If you are cooking, trying to speed up the time your pie spends in the oven will not help.

With this in mind, there are also things we can learn to be faster at or more productive with. If you have decided to write a book as one of your goals you may find that you type at an average speed of 40 words per minute. This is average. Not good, not bad; however, over time you will find that you can type faster and faster, which means the progress on your book will pick up speed. Then, instead of only writing 1,500 words in an hour, you can work that up to 2,750 words an hour.

If you have started woodworking for your Etsy shop, at first it may take you an hour to finish a product. But with time, new tools, and experience you will find yourself finishing six or more within the hour you are given.

I encourage the Power Hour Technique because it teaches us to work with less time, and encourages maximum productivity. Instead of taking time away from other responsibilities, you learn to use this time in the best way you can.

In fact, that is how I wrote this book! I insisted on putting aside an hour every day to write, then edit, and then format. At first, I could only write about a chapter a day, but by the end, I was writing 2–3 chapters every day, because I knew I only had so much time, and I needed to use the time well.

Making It Work

There are a lot of distractions in our lives that will seem to seep into our productivity and render our time useless. Sometimes our distractions are as simple as social media usage, but sometimes they are as complicated as our family needing our attention. How do you make this Power Hour work?

First and foremost, you need backup. Yes, you are calling in for backup. This hour is all about you, and that means no distractions. There are a few ways to do this so we are going to discuss your three best options.

Option #1 : The Early Bird Technique

I learned this technique from a woman who wanted to be an author and was working on her first fiction series. Everyone in her family had an early bedtime, and she knew that her best work would come to fruition in the early hours of the morning. She would wake up as early as 4 a.m. and get right to work on her manuscript. She knew that her youngest children would easily be awake by 6 a.m. so she scheduled in her hour well before they woke up so she could also start getting breakfast ready before everyone rolled out of bed.

This option is obviously not for everyone, but it can make it really easy to get your time in without taking time out of your normal day. This way there is no break in your family's schedule, and you get to work in the peace and quiet of the morning.

Option #2 : The Takeover Technique

This is my go-to technique, especially when I am pregnant and getting up early is hard. This is the most difficult technique to plan at first, but once you get into a habit it can be an awesome option for everyone in the family. First, you and your husband need to set aside your hour of the day. This could be the hour right after he gets home from work, or the hour following dinner time. (If you are a single mother, or your husband isn't available, this individual could also be a babysitter, mother, friend, etc.)

For this hour, Daddy is in charge of the kids. To make this work, my husband would take our children out of the house and they would get their exercise while I had peace and quiet. It would give me an opportunity to work with no distractions. Make it clear to your husband that this is his hour with the kids.

My kids love to have this hour with Dad after they have spent all day with Mom. It helps them solidify their relationship with their father. I need to note, this will only work if your husband is 100% on board, and he understands how important this hour is to you. If your husband would like a Power Hour as well, find a way to work it out together.

Option #3 : The Night Owl Technique

This option is for those of you who like staying up late. It is similar to the Early Bird technique, in that your husband will not need to take charge of the kids for you. You will simply take an hour after everyone has gone to bed and focus on your project.

This, in my opinion, is one of the most difficult options, because you are generally exhausted from your day's work. This means you do not have the energy or interest left to pursue your project; however, it will work wonders for some people.

I encourage you to try your different options before settling on one. That way you will know what works best for you and your family.

Time and Support From Your Spouse

Do you remember how we discussed at the beginning of the book that as a child you are very self-oriented and then as an adult that all changes? We learn that to be successful and happy we really need to become selfless.

Your children are in their "self" phase, and this is the perfect opportunity for you and your spouse to teach your children how to be selfless. Although you can explain the importance of this Power Hour to your children, it will be even more meaningful coming from your spouse.

When your husband takes charge of your kids so you can work on a project, your husband is being selfless. He can explain to your kids that, "Mom has spent all day keeping our home and our family happy and healthy, so now we have an opportunity to give mom one hour to work on her own project. Let's show mom how much we love her by being quiet, and letting her focus."

It may take time for your kids to understand what "being quiet" and "do not bother mom" entails, but over time they will learn to look outside of themselves and see how their actions affect mom during this time.

Hopefully, your spouse has learned that taking over the kids is a huge help in giving you time and support on this journey you are embarking on, but sometimes he may need a reminder. Remind him in a kind way. The best way is to thank him when he helps you.

It is not easy to come home from a long day at work, and immediately take over all of the home responsibilities. Thank him for his willingness to do that. Thank him for caring about you, and helping you achieve your dreams. A simple "thank you" can go a really long way. (A kiss doesn't hurt either!)

Just as you thank your husband for his help and support, thank your children for their help and support. It is hard to not go running to mom when they normally would. Thank them for holding back for that Power Hour.

Congratulate them when you have finished your Power Hour, and explain that they helped you get X-amount of things done today! They will feel so proud that they made such a big difference in mom's life, and that they were able to help.

Use Your Time Well

I am going to challenge you to take an hour tomorrow. Decide when you want that hour to occur, and decide what you would like to get done. For example:

"My Power Hour will start at 4 p.m. tomorrow, and I will create two new bracelets for my Etsy shop."

OR

"My Power Hour will start at 5 a.m. tomorrow, and I will write a complete outline for my book."

Whatever your goal, I want you to make it specific. After you have finished your Power Hour, I want you to consider what you can change about your process to make that hour even more productive. It is not simply about taking an hour every day to work, it is about using that hour the best way you can.

This practice will be a process of trial and error, but eventually you will get into the swing of things. You will know exactly what you are capable of. You will also learn what time of day is your best time to work.

This Power Hour Technique can also be applied across the board. Cleaning Power Hour? You betcha. How much cleaning can you get done in an hour? I think you would be surprised! Homework Power Hour? That can work too! Get everyone to sit down at the dining room table, start the timer, and challenge them to get as much work done as they can.

Learning to be fast and efficient is a byproduct of the Power Hour technique. Not only will it make a difference in your life, but it will also help your husband and children to accomplish similar things in their lives as well.

There are a lot of things to accomplish in this world. There are a lot of experiences to be had, a lot of things to learn, a lot of people to meet, and more! As you learn that every minute in your day counts, you will find that your days will have more and more possibilities than you ever imagined.

Sometimes I like to define days by a single activity, such as "the day we go to the zoo." Well, you might be taking a trip to the zoo that day, but will it take up all 12+ productive, wakeful hours you have available to you? That is not likely. If you generalize your day, that is a quick way to lose valuable time because you start to think that the generalization is the only activity happening that day.

Sure, some days will be for rest. In fact, I encourage Sunday to be one of those days for you. Take a break, relax, and enjoy being alive. Then when Monday comes around you are well-rested and ready to jump into your schedule.

THE HOMEMAKING HANDBOOK

ACTION PLAN

❐ Teach your spouse about the Power Hour technique. Explain to your children the Power Hour technique.

❐ Schedule in a Power Hour for yourself every day.

❐ Make a plan for what you will accomplish in your Power Hour every day.

14 : THE EIGHT ELEMENTS

We have discussed the eight elements and how they relate to your life overall, but I would like to take a deeper look at them on a personal level. We will also discuss some ideas for projects, goals, and aspirations you can work towards.

Some of these goals will fit into your Power Hour time, but some will simply be lifestyle changes that you will have to find ways to implement. For example: "eating healthy" is not an hour-a-day goal; however, "exercising regularly" could become an hour-a-day goal.

It is a really good idea to make a goal for yourself in each of these elements so that you are balancing out all aspects of your life. It is likely that you will not implement all of these goals at once. Instead, you will pick two to four goals that you would like to focus on. Later you will introduce new goals as you accomplish the others or make them part of your daily habits.

It is also good to remember moderation in all things. Sometimes we pour ourselves into something we love and leave things we need by the wayside. Over time the things we love will lose attention because we are forced to catch up with things we ignored. Some of the next few months may feel like you are pulling yourself out of a pit you dug, but I assure you it will be wonderfully rewarding as you take these baby steps to realizing your dreams.

Physical

Physical health is one of the facets of wellness where the two extremes are pretty obvious to the naked eye. There are absolute health nuts, and those who could not care less. On one end of the spectrum, an individual would diet and exercise regularly; on the other end, one would eat whatever they wanted and not bother with exercise. Then there is the infinite spectrum of individuals in between. No matter where you are on this spectrum it should be a part of your plan to maintain a healthy body.

We will break up goal examples into two categories. The General goal examples will be the hopes you have for yourself in the future. You will then make an action plan and those will become your Power Hour goals.

General Goal Examples:

Lose 15 pounds

Eradicate sugar from my diet

Learn to meal prep

Get enough rest

Run a marathon

Eat smaller food portions

Eat only natural foods

Power Hour Goal Examples:

Exercise and Stretch

Meal Plan & Meal Prep

Morning hygiene routine (shower, brush teeth, etc.)

Emotional

Emotional health can be approached from a number of places, but in general you must know how to deal with them and have healthy coping practices. This also includes having a healthy outlook despite disappointments and frustrating circumstances. Sometimes adopting a leisure activity can help us relax and regenerate. Sometimes meditation or writing in a journal can help us organize our feelings and thoughts.

Your emotional health practices, more than any other element, will be specific to you. Nobody knows, more than you, what helps you relax, clear your mind, and understand how different factors in your life affect your emotional well-being.

To get started on finding goals for your emotional health, start by examining stressors in your life. Next, consider ways that you can either eliminate those stressors or learn to live with them, and make them less stressful. Maybe you have a frustrating class you are required to take and you have learned that a quick jog afterwards helps relieve the stress and let you reset your emotions.

General Goal Examples:

Relieve stress

Meditate more often

Adopt a calming leisure activity

Strengthen my healthy relationships

Power Hour Goal Examples:

Walk a nearby trail

Take a relaxing bath

Listen to music while baking bread

Intellectual

I want to remind you that learning does not end with motherhood. We seem to catch ourselves in the trap of daily tasks and forget that our personal growth is just as important as our husband's and our children's. Some mothers find that they had stalled their personal learning opportunities for so long, that becoming an empty nester left them unsure of what their goals in life were.

Remember that learning goals are not necessarily educational goals. You do not have to constantly be working towards a degree to fulfill yourself intellectually. A great place to start is by considering talents that you are already blessed with, and to find ways to improve on those abilities. You could also look into interests you have never tried before, but always wanted to explore.

This is not to say that you should not pursue an education, it is simply to note that you do not need to invest money to learn and grow.

General Goal Examples:

Sign up for local classes

Learn a new skill

Learn a new language

Teach or tutor others

Power Hour Goal Examples:

Practice the piano

Spend an hour on Rosetta Stone

Take a painting class at the Rec Center

Read a book on gardening

Social

Your social well-being is all about the strength of your personal relationships and your social network. This is all about interaction and building friendships. If you are anything like me, this section may scare you. For more introverted people, this element can seem a little bit stressful, but there is no need for that.

What is important is building up the relationships we have, and having healthy interaction with those around us. You can also consider the impact that your involvement has on the community. This could extend to your neighborhood, your child's school, and more.

General Goal Examples

Improving my relationship with my sister

Joining a book club

Attend more social events

Get involved in my child's club sport

Power Hour Goal Examples

Have a weekly lunch date with my mother

Have a phone conversation with my father

Enjoy a date with my husband

Occupational

Occupational wellness will not directly apply to every mother, but that does not mean you cannot brainstorm some ideas for you personally, or your family in general. Maybe you have no interest in pursuing a career. That is okay. Sometimes our children have an interest in pursuing a business idea and we can learn to support them by learning what is required in running a business.

We can always try to learn with our children and join them on their journey, or we can attempt to grow our own family business. This does not need to be anything detailed and difficult. It can merely be an opportunity for family members to work, and for the family to have an extra income.

Obviously, this will apply to each family differently, and you and your husband will have to decide each other's responsibilities and how you will work to build a business. You will also need to make arrangements if you decide to build your own career and enter the workforce.

In all of these things, remember to gift yourself the time to build an occupation, but make sure that the needs of your home and family are also met.

General Goal Examples:

Create a vision board for your career goals

Build a business

Start a blog

Open an Etsy shop

Power Hour Goal Examples:

Manage tasks for your business

Build products that have been ordered

Design a new product

Make a business plan with your child

Environmental

Remember that we are not referring to environmental wellness in this book as "going green." It is simply about improving your living environment so that you can be happy and healthy. Your living environment is most likely your home.

Your home is your happiness. If the color of the paint bothers you, change the color of the paint. If you feel unsafe in your neighborhood, consider moving options and opportunities. If your couches are 25 years old and it grosses you out then invest in new couches.

Sometimes we will be forced to deal with difficult environments. While my husband was in law school we decided it was important to save money any way that we could. We ended up living in on-campus apartments. They were very small, the walls were cinderblock, and the bedrooms were more like closets.

It was REALLY difficult for me to enjoy this apartment, but it was more important for us to save money than to enjoy a luxury apartment. Whatever your situation, make sure you are only living in a difficult environment for temporary reasons, not for forever.

General Goal Examples:
> Keep the house clean
> Renovate the kitchen
> Redecorate the bedroom

Power Hour Goal Examples
> Organize the pantry
> Power cleaning session
> Build a bookshelf
> Repaint the bathroom

Spiritual

Spiritual wellness will be different for everyone. If you are religious, then a lot of your spiritual goals will stem from your religion. This could include creating a habit of praying and reading your scriptures.

THE HOMEMAKING HANDBOOK

It could also include attending church meetings or fulfilling a calling or job within your church.

Your spiritual goals will reflect your purpose in life. Why do you choose to do what you do? To have a strong spiritual health you must have clear views of your values, morals, and ethics. Volunteer work can play a huge part in our spiritual health it allows us to look outside of ourselves. Looking outside of yourself is a good beginning for spiritual wellness. If your purpose in life is focused on you then you may want to expand your vision. This is a very personal decision and feeling that you must work to understand your entire life.

General Goal Examples:

Become active in a church

Delve deeper into scriptures

Learn to be grateful

Explore religious or spiritual beliefs

Power Hour Goal Examples:

Attend a church meeting

Read scriptures

Go over a church lesson plan

Attend a church event

Meditate

Financial

Lastly, we are discussing financial wellness. There will not be a list for this section as I believe there is only one necessary action that will make a difference in your <u>personal</u> financial wellness.

Helpful Hint

It is a great idea to learn about retirement, saving, reducing debts, investing, and more; however, ideally this should be done with your spouse so that you are learning and making financial decisions together. If you would like to learn about these things, include it in your monthly budget meeting.

When you plan a budget with your family, a lot of financial wellness requirements will be covered for you individually. You should include a fun category in your budget for both you and your husband.

This means that every month, maybe you set aside $50 for you, and $50 for your spouse and that money is for you to use for YOU.

My husband would likely find a multi-player video game that we could enjoy together, and I would most likely waste my money on sushi. Let me reword: I would most likely delegate my money to sushi. If your purchase is good and it makes you happy, it is not a wasted purchase.

Often when we get married, we join together our incomes and

expenses and we give up the free spending money that we always took for granted. This Fun Fund gives you an opportunity to indulge in some personal interests that you do not necessarily share with your spouse, but will give you a little boost of happiness in purchasing.

CREATE A "FUN FUND."

ACTION PLAN

- ☐ Create a general goal in each element.
- ☐ Pick two to four goals to focus on.
- ☐ Break down each goal you have made into actionable, baby steps.

PART 5 : CONCLUSION

152

15 : MASTER PLAN

Throughout this book, I have encouraged you to question yourself about how you are currently living. I have also encouraged you to create your own action plans in each chapter. We are going to wrap up this book by applying everything we have covered and turn it into your own personal Master Plan.

1 : Goals

Call a family council and create a packet showcasing the family's goals and every family member's individual goals. If you have time and the resources, encourage every family member to create a vision board to showcase their goals. This will give everyone a reminder that they have something to work towards.

Make sure that you have a personal record of your goals, your husband's goals, and each child's goals so that you can work their dreams into the schedule.

Discuss the three Ts that are required for everyone's goals and ambitions to flourish: Tools. Time. Tribute.

2 : Schedule

It is time to create a working schedule. I suggest you purchase a large family calendar, where the month's plans, events, and expectations are all there for everyone to see. Create a weekly calendar (you can use the free downloadable packet) and create a separate weekly schedule for each member of your family.

Why should you do this? Each family member's schedule will be different. They participate in different sports, they may attend different schools, and they will have different responsibilities at home. If you are struggling to remember what to include in your schedule, refer to the scheduling section in Chapter 6.

When you approach your monthly schedule remember to include your council meetings, your family nights, your meal planning and grocery shopping, and your budget meetings.

3 : Responsibilities

Get clear on each family member's individual responsibilities. Know where everyone stands, and how they can help family life run smoothly.

4 : Get Clean

Make a cleaning plan. Know what chores need to be taken care of daily, weekly, monthly, and yearly. Make sure to keep a daily checklist out so your kids know what needs to be done. Do the same with your weekly expectations.

If this applies to you, set up chore charts, commission agreements, and cleaning expectations with your children. You can use the cleaning pages in our free download for inspiration.

Remember: Facilitate the cleaning of your home, and do not become the maid.

5 : Budget

Set up a budget based on your family's needs. Remember to allocate some money for you and your spouse's Fun Funds.

6 : Meal Plan

Plan your meals and grocery expectations for at least two weeks. After two weeks, reassess and make changes where necessary.

7 : Organize

Get your home in working order. Make sure to set up any activity stations that we discussed in Chapter 8. Make sure everyone knows where everything goes. If you need to color code your kitchen utensils, plates, and bowls, consider doing that.

8 : Reach Out

When all is said and done, fill in empty spaces of your schedule by finding ways to reach out to family and friends. Encourage good relationships, and help your children build strong relationships with their siblings and friends.

9 : Repeat

Put your plan into action.

It is a good idea to repeat the Master Plan process every quarter of the year. Make a plan to "Review Our Master Plan" every 3–6 months so that you are always on top of your family's needs.

16 : YOU ARE UNIQUE

There was a song that my elementary school taught its students. The principal used to play a recording of the song over the loudspeaker every morning. I am pretty sure our principal wrote the song for the students. There was a lot of repeating, but in the end, the song stated, "You're unique. You're a masterpiece. You're a real, live work of art."

Along with this song, the principal used to collect really cool rocks and paint them on his own time. He would give the rocks as gifts to students and remind them that every rock was different and beautiful in its own way. We were like those rocks. Different and beautiful.

Every mother is different. No two mothers will parent exactly the same way. Every wife is different. No two wives will be exactly the same. We are blessed with the agency to act in our own ways, and there is not another soul on earth that will make the exact same decisions as you in every situation.

This is a beautiful thing because what I look for in a husband will not be exactly the same as what you look for. If all men were exactly the same, we would not have a lot of variety to choose from. Remember that your spouse chose you because you are unique. If he did not believe you were a masterpiece, he would not have committed to loving you.

Our spouses know that we are learning and building ourselves as best as we can. They know we are not perfect, but they also know we are working to improve ourselves. If your spouse knows you purchased this book, then he knows you are trying to take steps to improve.

Rarely do our spouses have impossible expectations for us. In some cases their expectations can seem a little far-fetched. In those situations it is best to follow your intuition, and to know when you have done your best. In most cases it is likely that your spouse wants exactly what you want. They are also probably willing to help in whatever ways they can. But what do you want?

Would you like a happy, clean, and organized home? Would you like your family to look forward to returning home at the end of every day? Would you like to have the time and energy necessary to enjoy your family's company? Would you like to be able to wake up with the confidence that you will accomplish something valuable every day? I'm sure these are all dreams that you value, and it is likely that your spouse shares those dreams. He is your partner, and he only wants the best for himself, you, and your children. Take this journey together and you will see how amazing the hard work and determination of two people can be.

The Perfect Mother

There is no such thing as the perfect mother, not on this earth. As you have seen throughout the book, I do not instruct you on how exactly to implement my strategies. There is a good reason for this. One strategy will not work for everyone.

This is obvious, especially when you look at something as simple as a classroom. A teacher will implement a strategy and it will work perfectly for some students, then other students will still fail. Your husband and your children are as unique as you are. The strategies I have introduced to you here will only make so much of a difference if you do not cater them to your family's quirks.

My mother has always hated cleaning. She worked as a caretaker for an elderly couple at one point, and she would leave the house, drive out to their home, walk in, and begin her cleaning ritual. She knew that once she started cleaning it had to be finished so she pressed through.

After she quit working for this couple she found that she could implement the same strategy in her home. So, what did she do? She would wake up in the morning, put her shoes on, leave the house, come back as if she were going to work, and start her cleaning routine.

A lot of people may think…seriously? That's weird. But it worked for my mom! She could finish cleaning, chores, and any other tasks in her home by treating it as a workday. This helped her mindset.

You will find that as you experiment with this book there will be some quirks that work really well for you. You may even swear by them, but those same silly practices may not work for everyone. It does not mean that they are completely unique to you either.

Sometimes the trick is simply to follow a pattern. If I turn on Disney music in my home then I know it will keep my daughter occupied for long enough that I can clean all of the floors in our apartment without her trying to "help." So, every time I need to clean the floors, on comes the Disney music. Works like a charm.

Find your patterns that are healthy. If they are obvious enough, your children will learn to recognize them.

Keep in mind, you are working to master motherhood, not become the "perfect" mother. If becoming the perfect mother is your end goal, you will find that you fail 100/100 times. This process is not about perfection, it is about progress.

The Key Element

If there is one important element in your life that I find necessary to make your home, family, and yourself happy, it is LOVE. Love is the most important element.

Love your spouse, love your children, and love yourself.

The definition of love is to "like very much; find pleasure in." Find pleasure in your spouse, find pleasure in your children, and find pleasure in yourself. If you are constantly finding reasons to not find pleasure in these things then it is time to do some soul-searching.

I want to be clear, you can only fix yourself. Of course, you can encourage positive change in those around you, but you cannot change them. Learn instead to separate their positive characteristics from their flaws and find joy and pleasure in the positive aspects of their personality.

THE HOMEMAKING HANDBOOK

The more you find, recognize, and are grateful for these aspects, the more pleasurable aspects of their personalities will emerge. That same situation goes for you. Find the aspects of yourself that make you happy. Build on them, help them grow, and over time you will find that you have even more to offer your family, your home, and yourself than you ever thought possible.

162

ABOUT THE AUTHOR

Alina Lauren is the writer, designer, and founder of alinadampt.com, a company focused on offering quality resources for wives and mothers. What began as a personal challenge to continue her personal growth developed into an aid for other women in organizing their lives and accomplishing their dreams. An award-winning harpist and experienced dancer, Alina earned her BA in Dance Production and Management. She enjoys baking bread, taking walks, writing music, and spending time with her husband and children.

Printed in Great Britain
by Amazon